Just Enough
Dutch

Dennis Strik

Hugo's Language Books Limited

© 1996 Hugo's Language Books Ltd
All rights reserved
ISBN 0 85285 288 6

'Just Enough Dutch' is also available in a pack with two cassettes:
ISBN 0 85285 289 4

Written by
Dennis Strik

Edited by
Jenny Yoboué

Illustrations by Sonia Robinson

Set in Palatino and Optima by
Keyset Composition, Colchester, Essex

Printed and bound in Great Britain by
Scotprint

Contents

Preface

Welcome to Hugo's **Just Enough Dutch**, a short course designed for busy people who want to be able to communicate effectively in Dutch when travelling abroad.

In the first chapter we give you basic grounding in Dutch pronunciation, which you should read through first of all, using the cassettes for extra guidance, if possible.

The remaining chapters offer the following:

- realistic dialogues using everyday language, with English translation;
- language notes, headed 'How it Works', to help you formulate what you want to say;
- useful information and tips on various aspects of Dutch life in the 'Streetwise' sections;
- exercises, headed 'Your Turn', with answers in the Key;
- a Word List of new vocabulary learnt in the chapter.

At the back of the book you will also find a Mini-Dictionary for quick reference.

We strongly recommend that you use the **Just Enough Dutch** cassettes in conjunction with this book, as you will find these invaluable for learning the correct pronunciation, although the book can be used on its own.

We hope that you enjoy **Just Enough Dutch**, and wish you good luck with your studies.

1 Pronunciation and Spelling

One of the most important aspects of learning a language is mastering the pronunciation. Your skills in speaking a language will only be put to effective use if people can understand the sounds you're making!

The best way of learning correct Dutch pronunciation is by imitating good Dutch speakers. The easiest way of doing this when you are learning the language on your own at home, is by listening to the cassettes that accompany this course. Listen carefully to the Dutch speakers on the cassette and repeat and imitate their pronunciation until you can make the sounds in exactly the same way.

As in English, stress falls on the first syllable of words in Dutch. But Dutch intonation differs from English, and the best way of acquiring this is to expose yourself to as much spoken Dutch as possible. If you have the opportunity, try to listen to Dutch radio and watch Dutch television.

CONSONANTS

The consonants of Dutch won't be much of a problem to speakers of English, as they're generally pronounced in the same way. Here are the main exceptions:

ch **zacht** *soft*, **macht** *power*, **licht** *light*
As in the Scottish '*loch*'. You should feel this at the back of your mouth (it won't hurt!).

g **gek** *mad*, **geel** *yellow*, **goed** *good*
The same guttural sound as **ch** above. A Dutch **g** is never pronounced as in English.

j **ja** *yes*, **jaar** *year*, **jong** *young*
As English '*y*' in '*yes*'.

5

k, p, t	**pop** *doll*, **tak** *branch*, **kat** *cat*

The same as in English but without exhaling as much air (when holding your hand in front of your mouth you should feel no air coming out with the Dutch words).

r   **rood** *red*, **roos** *rose*, **raar** *strange*

Made either by trilling your tongue against the back of your upper teeth or by making friction at the back of the mouth (like a French 'r').

sch   **school** *school*, **schip** *ship*, **schoon** *clean*

This is a combination of 's' and 'ch'.

v   **vis** *fish*, **ver** *far*, **vet** *fat*

Like English 'v' in 'give', but sometimes closer to English 'f' especially at the beginning of words.

w   **wit** *white*, **wip** *see-saw*

Between English 'v' and 'w'. Hold bottom teeth against upper lip.

VOWELS

The Dutch vowels are more difficult than the consonants because they differ considerably from those in English. There are short vowel sounds, long vowel sounds and combinations of vowels.

Short vowel sounds

a   **man** *man*, **pan** *pan*, **bal** *ball*

As in 'hard' but shorter.

e   **gek** *crazy*, **fles** *bottle*, **lek** *leak*

As in 'set' but shorter.

i   **wit** *white*, **mis** *mass*, **lip** *lip*

As in 'bit' but shorter.

o   **mop** *joke*, **rol** *role*, **bot** *bone*

As in 'hot' but shorter.

u   **kus** *kiss*, **bus** *bus*, **mus** *sparrow*

Similar to 'dirt' but shorter.

Long vowel sounds

aa   **kaas** *cheese*, **straat** *street*, **maan** *moon*

As in 'cat' but longer.

ee	**been** *leg*, **steen** *stone*, **leek** *layman*
	As in '*lane*'.
eu	**neus** *nose*, **keus** *choice*, **deur** *door*, **geur** *smell*
	No equivalent in English. Try making a vowel sound as in '*dirt*' and rounding your lips tightly.
ie	**niet** *not*, **dier** *animal*
	As in '*cheat*'.
oe	**boek** *book*, **koek** *gingerbread*
	As in '*book*' but with lips more rounded.
oo	**boos** *angry*, **boot** *boat*
	As in '*boat*'.
uu	**vuur** *fire*, **muur** *wall*
	No equivalent in English. Try making a vowel sound as in '*boot*' and purse your lips.

◉ COMBINATIONS OF VOWELS

au/ou	**blauw** *blue*, **oud** *old*
	No equivalent in English. Try making vowel sound as in '*shout*' but start by rounding lips more with mouth wide open.
aai	**saai** *boring*, **baai** *tough*
	Combination of **aa** and **ie**.
eeuw	**leeuw** *lion*, **eeuw** *century*
	Combination of **ee** and **oe**.
ei/ij	**trein** *train*, **dijk** *dike*
	No equivalent in English. In between English vowel sounds in '*night*' and '*late*'.
ieuw	**nieuw** *new*
	Combination of **ie** and **oe**.
oei	**groei** *growth*, **doei** *bye*
	Combination of **oe** and **ie**.
ooi	**mooi** *beautiful*, **kooi** *cage*
	Combination of **oo** and **ie**.
ui	**huis** *house*, **tuin** *garden*
	No equivalent in English. Try making English vowel sounds as in '*house*' and rounding lips tightly with tongue against bottom teeth.
uw	**ruw** *rough*, **sluw** *sly*
	Combination of **uu** and **oe**.

7

There is one other Dutch vowel sound which is similar to the English vowel sound in '*sist<u>er</u>*'. This sound can be spelt in different ways:

e as in **de** *the*   *de (french)*   **i** as in **aardig** *nice* *aardlike*
ee as in **een** *a*   *een. (french)*   **ij** as in **lelijk** *ugly*   *leyluck*

SPELLING

Dutch spelling is relatively straightforward. There is only one major rule to learn. This concerns the vowel sounds **a, e, o, u**

In the section on short vowel sounds which are spelt with one letter we saw:

man *man*   **lek** *leak*   **bot** *bone*   **mus** *sparrow*

These vowel sounds are always spelt with one letter and always occur in a closed syllable.

In the second section we saw long vowel sounds which are spelt with two letters:

maan *moon*   **leek** *layman*   **boot** *boat*   **muur** *wall*

These vowel sounds can be spelt either with two letters or one (**aa/a, ee/e, oo/o, uu/u**) depending on whether they appear in a closed or in an open syllable. (A closed syllable ends in a consonant. An open syllable ends in a vowel.)

The long vowel sounds above were spelt with double letters because they all appeared in closed syllables:

maan *moon*, **been** *leg*, **boot** *boat*, **vuur** *fire*

However, when the same sounds appear in an open syllable, they are spelt with a single letter. This happens, for instance, when **-en** is added to make words plural:

<u>ma</u>**nen** *moons*, <u>le</u>**ken** *laymen*, <u>bo</u>**ten** *boats*, <u>mu</u>**ren** *walls*

When **-en** is added the first syllable (underlined) becomes an open syllable and consequently the long vowel sound is spelt with one letter only. This is straightforward enough, although you may well wonder what to do if you want to make **man**

man plural. There is a simple solution to this problem: the consonant is doubled.

man *man*   **ma<u>nn</u>en** *men*

The two consonants make sure the syllable with the short vowel sound is closed (one **n** goes with the first and one with the last syllable: **man-nen**).

For the full picture, have a look at this table:

singular	plural		singular	plural	
man	**mannen**	*man*	**bot**	**botten**	*bone*
maan	**manen**	*moon*	**boot**	**boten**	*boat*
lek	**lekken**	*leak*	**mus**	**mussen**	*sparrow*
leek	**leken**	*layman*	**muur**	**muren**	*wall*

YOUR TURN

Exercise 1

Listen to the cassette and repeat the words recorded from this chapter.

Exercise 2

Without looking at the answers below, make the following words plural by adding **-en** and changing the spelling where necessary.

1. **beer** *bear*
2. **tuin** *garden*
3. **pen** *pen*
4. **kaart** *card*
5. **lip** *lip*
6. **stoel** *chair*
7. **buur** *neighbour*
8. **raam** *window*
9. **vrouw** *woman*
10. **man** *man*

KEY

Exercise 2

1. beren; 2. tuinen; 3. pennen; 4. kaarten; 5. lippen; 6. stoelen; 7. buren; 8. ramen; 9. vrouwen; 10. mannen

2 At the Hotel

On arrival in The Netherlands one of the first things you will have to do is arrange your accommodation. In these dialogues various people are booking a hotel room.

EEN KAMER ALSTUBLIEFT

Reception: Goedemorgen meneer.
Good morning, sir.
Guest: Goedemorgen, een kamer alstublieft. Voor drie nachten.
Good morning, a room, please. For three nights.
Reception: Met douche en toilet?

With shower and toilet?

Guest: Ja, graag.
Yes, please.

Reception: Wat is uw naam?
What is your name, please?

Guest: Mijn naam is Stone.
My name is Stone.

Reception: Prima meneer Stone, u heeft kamer zeventien. Dit is de sleutel.
Very well, Mr Stone, you are in room 17. Here is the key.

Guest: Dank u wel.
Thank you.

IK WIL GRAAG ...

Reception: Goedemiddag, mevrouw.
Good afternoon, madam.

Guest: Goedemiddag, ik wil graag een kamer.
Good afternoon, I would like a room, please.

Reception: Even kijken mevrouw. Wilt u een eenpersoonskamer of een tweepersoonskamer?
I'll have a look, madam. Would you like a single or a double?

Guest: Een eenpersoonskamer alstublieft.
A single, please.

Reception: Met douche en toilet?
With shower and toilet?

Guest: Nee, zonder douche en toilet.
No, without shower and toilet.

Reception: Voor hoeveel nachten?
For how many nights?

Guest: Voor zeven nachten.
For seven nights.

Reception: Dat kan, we hebben een mooie kamer met balkon voor u.
That's fine, we have a nice room with balcony for you.

Guest: Hoeveel kost de kamer?
How much does the room cost?

Reception: Honderd gulden per nacht, inclusief ontbijt.
One hundred guilders per night, including breakfast.

Guest: Prima, die neem ik.
Wonderful, I'll take that one.

WE ZOEKEN ...

Reception: Kan ik u helpen?
Can I help you?
Guest: Ja, we zoeken twee eenpersoonskamers
Yes, we'd like two single rooms.
Reception: Het spijt me, we hebben geen eenpersoonskamers.
I am sorry, we don't have any single rooms.
Guest: Hoeveel is een tweepersoonskamer?
How much is a double room?
Reception: Vijftig gulden per nacht per persoon voor een
kamer zonder bad of toilet.
*Fifty guilders per person per night for a room without bath
or toilet.*
Guest: Inclusief ontbijt?
Including breakfast?
Reception: Nee, exclusief ontbijt.
No, excluding breakfast.
Guest: Dat is goed. Accepteert u cheques?
That's all right. Do you accept cheques?
Reception: Nee, we accepteren geen cheques, alleen cash of
creditcards.
No, we don't accept cheques, only cash or credit cards.

EEN PROBLEEM

Reception: Kan ik u helpen?
Can I help you?
Guest: Ja, mijn kamer heeft geen douche en geen toilet.
Yes, my room doesn't have a shower and toilet.
Reception: Wat is het probleem?
What is the problem?
Guest: Ik heb een reservering voor een kamer met douche
en toilet.
I reserved a room with shower and toilet.
Reception: Er is een badkamer op de gang, meneer.

There is a bathroom in the corridor, sir.
Guest: Maar ik wil een kamer met douche en toilet.
But I want a room with shower and toilet.
Reception: Er is geen kamer met douche en toilet vrij. Ik heb
alleen een kamer met bad.
I'm afraid there isn't a room with shower and toilet
available. I only have a room with bath.
Guest: Ik wil geen bad, ik wil een douche en toilet!
I don't want a bath, I want a shower and toilet!

HOW IT WORKS

MAKING STATEMENTS IN DUTCH

Saying things in Dutch is often done in much the same way
as in English. Have a look at these examples from the
dialogues:

mijn naam is Jonker   *my name is Jonker*
dit is de sleutel   *this is the key*
ik wil een kamer   *I would like a room*

REQUESTING INFORMATION

Asking a question is easier in Dutch than in English because
no extra words like 'do you' are necessary. You simply put
the verb at the beginning of the sentence:

wilt u een kamer?   *do you want a room?*
accepteert u cheques?   *do you accept cheques?*

Keeping these examples in mind, simple sentences can easily
be turned into questions; just put the verb at the beginning of
the sentence:

statement: question:
de kamer heeft een douche   **heeft de kamer een douche?**
the room has a shower   *does the room have a shower?*
de prijs is inclusief ontbijt   **is de prijs inclusief ontbijt?**
the price is inclusive of breakfast *is the price inclusive of breakfast?*
zijn naam is Kees   **is zijn naam Kees?**
his name is Kees.   *is his name Kees?*

Questions starting with who?, what?, where? and how much? are formed and used in much the same way in Dutch as in English.

wie is dat?	*who is that?*
wat is uw naam?	*what is your name?*
waar is het station?	*where is the station?*
hoeveel kost de kamer?	*how much is the room?*

DE, HET, EEN

In Dutch there is only one word for *a* and *an*: **een**. This means you can never go wrong since it is always the same!

een kamer	*a room*
een Engelsman	*an Englishman*
een douche	*a shower*

Unfortunately, the Dutch equivalent of *the* is a little more complicated as there are two different words: **de** and **het**.

de kamer	*the room*
het hotel	*the hotel*
de vakantie	*the holiday*
het museum	*the museum*

With most words it is impossible to tell whether they are **de** or **het** words, which means you will have to learn them by heart. As there are far fewer **het** words than **de** words, the easiest way of going about this is to assume all words are **de** words and to learn the **het** words specifically. So you can guess **vakantie** (because it is a **de** word) but you will have to learn **het museum**.

MORE THAN ONE

When you look up a word in the vocabulary list or a dictionary, it will refer to a single item (singular). If you want to talk about more than one item (plural) – *rooms* and *hotels* – you can add an **-s** to many Dutch words, just like you do in English: **kamers** and **hotels**. Here are some examples using words from the dialogues.

singular:		plural:
balkon	–	**balkons**
sleutel	–	**sleutels**
creditcard	–	**creditcards**

However, there are some words which have a different ending, like *child* and *children* in English. You can add **-en** to some Dutch words but, just as in English, other forms also exist (think of *woman* and *women*). Again, you will simply have to learn this by heart. Here are some words you have already seen.

singular:		plural:
nacht	–	**nachten**
persoon	–	**personen**
museum	–	**musea**
naam	–	**namen**

Note that words referring to more than one item are always **de** words, even if they were **het** words originally. **Het hotel**, for instance, becomes **de hotels**, and **het museum** becomes **de musea**.

GEEN

In the third dialogue we saw that **geen** means *not any*:

het spijt me, we hebben geen eenpersoonskamers
I'm sorry, we don't have any single rooms

Geen often replaces **een**, as you can see from these examples:

we hebben een kamer	**we hebben geen kamer**
we have a room	*we do not have a room*
ik wil een douche	**ik wil geen douche**
I would like a shower	*I do not want a shower*
we accepteren cheques	**we accepteren geen cheques**
we accept cheques	*we do not accept cheques*

NUMBERS

Here are the numbers from one to twenty:

1	een	11	elf
2	twee	12	twaalf
3	drie	13	dertien
4	vier	14	veertien
5	vijf	15	vijftien
6	zes	16	zestien
7	zeven	17	zeventien
8	acht	18	achttien
9	negen	19	negentien
10	tien	20	twintig

And for good measure we should not forget zero!

0	nul

HOW TO ...

Ask for a hotel room

een kamer alstublieft	*a room please*
ik wil graag een kamer	*I would like a room*
we zoeken een kamer	*we are looking for a room*
ik zoek een kamer	*I am looking for a room*

Give information

mijn naam is Ayers	*my name is Ayers*
ik heb een reservering	*I have a reservation*
een kamer met toilet	*a room with toilet*
een kamer zonder douche	*a room without shower*

Request information

hoeveel kost de kamer?	*how much does the room cost?*
accepteert u cheques?	*do you accept cheques?*

Complain about your room

de kamer heeft geen toilet	*the room doesn't have a toilet*
de kamer heeft geen bad	*the room doesn't have a bath*
de kamer heeft geen douche	*the room doesn't have a shower*

STREETWISE

The Netherlands are bordered by the sea in the west and the north, by Germany in the east and by Belgium in the south. However you travel to The Netherlands you will have to pass **de douane**, *customs*. When travelling by road this will be at **de grens**, *the border*, with Germany or Belgium; when travelling by boat this will be the port of arrival (usually **Hoek van Holland**) and by plane it will be at **het vliegveld**, *the airport* (usually **Schiphol**). Although increasingly fewer checks are being carried out, thanks to the 'Schengen Agreement', EU citizens do need a valid **paspoort**, *passport*, to enter the country.

ACCOMMODATION

There are various kinds of **accommodatie**, *accommodation*. Hotels are usually available in every price range, particularly in the larger cities. **Jeugdherbergen**, *youth hostels*, are a cheap option for young people and can be found both in the cities (often simply called **youth hostels** there) and in rural areas. Camping is also popular in The Netherlands and numerous camp sites, called **campings**, can be found throughout the country. **Logies met ontbijt**, *bed and breakfast*, is not quite as popular in The Netherlands as it is in the UK but it does exist, particularly in smaller towns in tourist areas. People offering B&B will usually have a sign in the window saying **kamer vrij**, *room free*.

When planning a stay in a busy area or city, particularly during the summer, it may be advisable to make a reservation, **de reservering**, for your accommodation. This is easily done by telephone but remember that **een borg**, *a deposit*, may be required and that foreign cheques are not accepted everywhere. Your safest bet will therefore be to pay by **creditcard**.

YOUR TURN

Exercise 1

Listen to the dialogues recorded on the cassettes, without reading the book, and repeat the guests' lines in the gaps.

Exercise 2

Complete the following dialogue. You have just arrived in The Netherlands and want to book a hotel room. Listen to the receptionist recorded on the '*Just Enough Dutch*' cassettes and give your reply in the gaps.

Receptionist: Goedemorgen, kan ik u helpen?
You: [say you would like a room]
Receptionist: Een eenpersoonskamer of een tweepersoonskamer?
You: [say you would like a single and ask if the room has a shower]
Receptionist: Ja, het is een kamer met douche en toilet.
You: [ask how much the room is]
Receptionist: De kamer kost honderd gulden per nacht.
You: [ask whether breakfast is included]
Receptionist: Ja, de prijs is inclusief ontbijt.

Exercise 3

Make the following sentences into questions. Remember to put the verb first (see 'How it works'). Example:

1. De kamer heeft een toilet.
   question: Heeft de kamer een toilet?
2. De kamer heeft een douche.
3. De kamer heeft een balkon.
4. De kamer kost 20 gulden.
5. Zijn naam is Johan.
6. Hij wil een kamer.
7. Het ontbijt is inclusief.
8. De kamer heeft geen douche.

Exercise 4

Fill in the missing words:

1. Drie . . . [single rooms] voor zeven . . . [nights].
2. We accepteren geen . . . [credit cards].

3. Ik heb twee . . . [keys] voor de kamer.
4. Het hotel heeft ook . . . [double rooms].
5. Er zijn veel . . . [museums] in België en Nederland.
6. Hoeveel . . . [rooms] heeft het hotel?

Exercise 5

A. Read Exercise 4 out loud and listen to the cassette to check your pronunciation.
B. Say the following numbers out loud for practice:
   4, 7, 13, 8, 1, 20, 19, 14, 11, 9, 2, 15, 6.

Exercise 6

You are not satisfied with the hotel you are staying in and are trying to complain about it to the receptionist.

Tell the receptionist what you think is wrong:

1. the room doesn't have a toilet;
2. the room doesn't have a shower;
3. the room doesn't have a balcony.
4. Then say you have a reservation for a room with a toilet, shower and balcony and that (5) you want a room with all those things.

WORD LIST

het bad	bath
de badkamer	bathroom
het balkon	balcony
de bank	bank
de douche	shower
de eenpersoonskamer	single room
exclusief	excluding
de gang	corridor
de gulden	guilder
inclusief	including
ja	yes
de kamer	room
meneer	sir
mevrouw	madam
de naam	name
de nacht	night
het ontbijt	breakfast
ook	also
de persoon	person
prima	very well/fine

de prijs	price
het probleem	problem
de reservering	reservation
de sleutel	key
het toilet	toilet
de tweepersoonskamer	double room
veel	many

USEFUL EXPRESSIONS

dank u wel	thank you
er is	there is ...
er zijn	there are ...
goedemiddag	good afternoon
goedemorgen	good morning
het spijt me	I am sorry
hoeveel kost de kamer?	how much does the room cost?
ik wil graag ...	I would like ...
ja graag	yes please
kan ik u helpen?	can I help you?
met bad/douche/toilet	with bath/shower/toilet
mijn naam is ...	my name is ...
per nacht	per night
per persoon	per person
zonder bad/douche/toilet	without bath/shower/toilet

KEY

Exercise 2

Note: the answers given here are examples and are by no means the only possible answers.

- Goedemorgen, een kamer alstublieft.
- Een eenpersoonskamer alstublieft. Heeft de kamer een douche?
- Hoeveel kost de kamer?
- Inclusief ontbijt?

Exercise 3

2. Heeft de kamer een douche? 3. Heeft de kamer een balkon?
4. Kost de kamer 20 gulden? 5. Is zijn naam Johan? 6. Wil hij een kamer? 7. Is het ontbijt inclusief? 8. Heeft de kamer geen douche?

Exercise 4

1. eenpersoonskamers, nachten. 2. creditcards. 3. sleutels.
4. tweepersoonskamers. 5. musea. 6. kamers.

Exercise 5(B)

vier; zeven; dertien; acht; een; twintig; negentien; veertien; elf;
negen; twee; vijftien; zes.

Exercise 6

1. De kamer heeft geen toilet. 2. De kamer heeft geen douche.
3. De kamer heeft geen balkon. 4. Ik heb een reservering voor een
kamer met toilet, douche en balkon. 5. Ik wil een kamer met toilet,
douche en balkon.

3 In a Bar

One of the first things you might want to do when arriving in Holland is to have a drink in a bar, and talk to people.

MIJN NAAM IS ...

Peter: Hallo, mijn naam is Peter Groot.
Hello, my name is Peter Groot.
David: Hallo, ik ben David Lane.
Hello, I'm David Lane.
Peter: Waar kom je vandaan?
Where are you from?
David: Ik kom uit Engeland, uit Londen.
I'm from England, from London.

Peter: Ben je op vakantie in Nederland?
Are you on holiday in The Netherlands?

David: Ja, met mijn vriendin. We zijn twee weken op vakantie.
Yes, with my girlfriend. We are on holiday for two weeks.

Peter: Hoe heet je vriendin?
What is your girlfriend called?

David: Ze heet Linda.
She is called Linda.

⊙⊙ HOE HEET JE?

Nick: Hallo, hoe heet je?
Hello, what is your name?

Karin: Ik heet Karin, en jij?
My name is Karin, what's yours?

Nick: Ik heet Nick. Ik kom uit Schotland. Waar kom jij vandaan?
My name is Nick. I'm from Scotland. Where are you from?

Karin: Ik kom uit Nederland. Ik woon in Den Haag.
I'm from The Netherlands. I live in The Hague.

Nick: Wil je iets drinken?
Would you like a drink?

Karin: Ja, lekker.
Yes, that would be nice.

Nick: Wat wil je?
What would you like?

Karin: Een biertje alsjeblieft.
A beer, please.

Bartender: Goedenavond, zeg het maar.
Good evening, what would you like?

Nick: Twee bier graag.
Two beers, please.

Bartender: Dat is vier vijfenzeventig alsjeblieft.
That's f4,75, please.

Nick: Alsjeblieft.
There you are.

Bartender: Dank je wel.
Thanks.

23

(• •) PRETTIG KENNIS TE MAKEN

Langhuizen: Goedemiddag, mijn naam is Langhuizen. Wat is uw naam?
Good afternoon, my name is Langhuizen. What is your name?

Jansen: Mijn naam is Jansen. Prettig kennis te maken.
My name is Jansen. Pleased to meet you.

Langhuizen: Wilt u iets drinken?
Would you like a drink?

Jansen: Ja, graag.
Yes, please.

Bartender: Zegt u het maar.
What would you like?

Langhuizen: Twee rode wijn, alstublieft.
Two red wines, please.

Bartender: Dat is vijf vijftig.
That's f5,50.

Langhuizen: Alstublieft.
There you are.

Bartender: Dank u wel.
Thank you.

(• •) IK BEN ...

Emilie: Ik ben Emilie. Ben jij Rob?
I am Emilie. Are you Rob?

Alex: Nee, ik ben Alex.
No, I am Alex.

Emilie: Wat is je achternaam?
What is your last name?

Alex: Mijn achternaam is Thislewood.
My last name is Thislewood.

Emilie: Kun je dat spellen?
Could you spell that?

Alex: Ja, T–H–I–S–L–E–W–O–O–D.
Yes, T–H–I–S–L–E–W–O–O–D.

24

MAG IK ... ?

Bartender:	Kan ik u helpen?
	Can I help you?
Customer:	Ja, mag ik twee witte wijn?
	Yes, two white wines, please.
Bartender:	Natuurlijk ... Komt u uit Nederland?
	But of course ... Are you from The Netherlands?
Customer:	Nee, ik kom uit Engeland. Ik ben op vakantie in Nederland met mijn vrouw.
	No, I am from England. I am on holiday in The Netherlands with my wife.
Bartender:	Hier is de wijn, dat is zeven gulden.
	Here is the wine. That is f7.
Customer:	Alstublieft.
	There you are.
Bartender:	Dank u wel en een prettige vakantie!
	Thank you and have a nice holiday!

IK KOM UIT ...

Piet:	Kom je uit Nederland?
	Are you from The Netherlands?
Anne:	Nee, ik kom uit Canada.
	No, I am from Canada.
Piet:	Wat is je naam?
	What is your name?
Anne:	Mijn naam is Anne.
	My name is Anne.
Piet:	Ben je op vakantie?
	Are you on holiday?
Anne:	Ja, met mijn vriend, hij komt ook uit Canada en zijn naam is Ted.
	Yes, with my boyfriend. He is also from Canada and his name is Ted.

25

HOW IT WORKS

IK, JIJ, U, HIJ, ZIJ ...

You will have noticed that you use **ik** to talk about yourself in Dutch, just as you use *I* in English. You may also have noticed that you use **je**, **jij** or **u** if you are addressing someone else and **hij** or **zij** if you are talking about another person. There are also equivalents for the English *we*, *you* (plural) and *they*. All these words are used just as they are in English.

singular:

ik	*I*
jij (je)	*you* (informal)
u	*you* (formal)
hij	*he*
zij (ze)	*she*
het	*it*

plural:

wij (we)	*we*
jullie (je)	*you* (informal)
u	*you* (formal)
zij (ze)	*they*

As you can see, **jij**, **zij**, **wij**, **jullie** and **zij** have an alternative form, given in brackets. You should normally use this form, and only use **jij**, **zij**, **wij** etc. for emphasis. Compare **je** and **jij** in the following sentences.

woon je in Amsterdam?
do you live in Amsterdam?

ik woon in Amsterdam, waar woon jij?
I live in Amsterdam, where do you live?

There are two different words for *you* in both the singular and in the plural. You choose between these according to the formality of the situation. **Jij**, **je** and **jullie** are used with friends and relatives, i.e. in very informal situations and **u** is used with strangers and superiors. So, you might ask a friend: **ben je moe?** (*are you tired?*) But a stranger would be addressed as **u**: **wie bent u?** (*who are you?*).

TO BE OR NOT TO BE

In the dialogues we have already seen several different forms of the verb **zijn**, *to be*, and we have also seen different situations in which to use this verb. You can use **zijn** to introduce yourself:

ik <u>ben</u> William

You can introduce others with **zijn**:

dit <u>is</u> Ted

Zijn can be used to ask other people to introduce themselves:

wie <u>bent</u> u?

and **zijn** can also be used to say something about yourself:
ik <u>ben</u> op vakantie

The verb **zijn** is used so often that it is a good idea to learn it by heart. Below you will find all the different forms.

zijn	*to be*

singular:

ik ben	*I am*
jij bent	*you are* (informal)
u bent	*you are* (formal)
hij/zij/het is	*he/she/it is*

plural:

wij zijn	*we are*
jullie zijn	*you are* (informal)
u bent	*you are* (formal)
zij zijn	*they are*

Note what happens to **jij ben<u>t</u>** when you ask a question:
ben jij Rob? ben je moe?

The **t**-ending is lost when the verb is put in front of **jij/je**. This happens to all verbs:

je kom<u>t</u> uit Nederland, but **kom je uit Nederland?**

Note that in **hoe heet jij?**, the **-t** is not an ending, it is part of the verb.

THE ALPHABET

Abroad, your name will sound unfamiliar to many people, so it will be useful if you can spell it in Dutch, to avoid confusion. Below you will find the Dutch alphabet to help you do this, together with imitated pronunciation in English. The best way of getting the pronunciation right, as always, is to listen to a Dutch person, so use the cassettes and try to repeat the sounds as accurately as possible.

A	ah	H	hah	O	oh	V	fay/vay
B	bay	I	ee	P	pay	W	vay
C	say	J	yay	Q	kee	X	iks
D	day	K	kah	R	air	Y	ee-grek
E	ay	L	ell	S	ess	Z	zett
F	eff	M	emm	T	tay		
G	hgay	N	enn	U	*ee* (but with rounded lips)		

MORE NUMBERS

In the previous chapter we learnt the numbers 1 to 20. Now we will look at the numbers from 20 to 100.

20	**twintig**	25	**vijfentwintig**
21	**eenentwintig**	26	**zesentwintig**
22	**tweeëntwintig**	27	**zevenentwintig**
23	**drieëntwintig**	28	**achtentwintig**
24	**vierentwintig**	29	**negenentwintig**
30	**dertig**	70	**zeventig**
40	**veertig**	80	**tachtig**
50	**vijftig**	90	**negentig**
60	**zestig**	100	**honderd**

Combined numbers between 20 and 99 are all made like the examples with 20 above: the last number first, then **en** and then the first number. Some examples:

34	**vierendertig**	97	**zevenennegentig**
68	**achtenzestig**	72	**tweeënzeventig**
45	**vijfenveertig**	89	**negenentachtig**

The two dots over some of the 'e's are called *trema* and indicate that a new syllable starts on this letter.

HOW TO ...

Introduce yourself

mijn naam is ...	*my name is ...*
ik heet ...	*my name is/I am ...*
ik ben ...	*I am ...*

Say where you are from

ik kom uit ...	*I am from ...*
ik woon in ...	*I live in ...*

Ask someone what he or she is called

Informal:

wat is je naam?	*what is your name?*
hoe heet je?	*what is your name?*
ben jij ... ?	*are you ... ?*

Formal:

wat is uw naam?	*what is your name?*
hoe heet u?	*what is your name?*
bent u ... ?	*are you ... ?*

Ask someone where he or she is from

Informal:

waar kom je vandaan?	*where are you from?*
waar woon je?	*where do you live?*

Formal:

waar komt u vandaan?	*where are you from?*
waar woont u?	*where do you live?*

Say thank you

Informal:

dank je wel	*thank you*
bedankt	*thanks*

Formal:

dank u wel	*thank you*

Offer to get someone a drink

Informal:

wil je iets drinken?	*would you like a drink?*

Formal:

wilt u iets drinken?	*would you like a drink?*

Order a drink
Formal and Informal:

een bier, graag	*a beer, please*
mag ik een vodka?	*could I have a vodka?*

Informal:

een biertje, alsjeblieft	*one beer, please*

Formal:

twee appelsap, alstublieft	*two apple juices, please*

When ordering one beer you can use both **een bier** or **een biertje**. Both are perfectly all right, but **biertje** is more informal and makes your order sound more casual (**biertje** literally means 'small beer').

Note that in Dutch, unlike in English, the drink that you are ordering always remains singular, even if you are ordering more than one. '*Two beers*', for instance, is **twee bier** in Dutch. Here are

some more examples:

drie whisky	*three whiskies*
twee sinaasappelsap	*two orange juices*

STREETWISE

SOCIAL MANNERS

Although introducing yourself or greeting people in Dutch is straightforward enough, and in many ways the same as in other Western European countries, some elements of the procedure are a little different. You always shake each other's hand – both upon arrival and when saying goodbye – and if you know each other well enough to kiss you should kiss each other on the cheek three times! This might seem a little excessive but it's the most normal thing to the Dutch.

Shaking hands and kissing is all part of the Dutch aim to make life **gezellig**, to make every situation as pleasant, amiable and enjoyable as possible. A social gathering is only successful if it's **gezellig**, which means chatting freely and being relatively relaxed and informal with each other. An important place is reserved for **koffiedrinken**, *drinking coffee*. The Dutch drink **koffie**, *coffee*, all day, for breakfast, during special **koffiepauzes,** *coffee breaks,* in the morning, for lunch, in the afternoon and after dinner. They take their **koffie met of zonder suiker en melk,** *with or without sugar and milk,* and they also drink **koffie verkeerd,** *milky coffee,* **cappuccino** and **espresso.**

When engaged in social conversation with the Dutch you will generally find them friendly and open, but beware of two things. Firstly, the Dutch will always try and make you speak English. Persevere! Make it clear that it is much harder for you to get practice in speaking Dutch than it is for them to practise speaking English. Insist that you really want to learn the language and that you need their help. Be friendly but firm! Secondly, beware of Dutch frankness. You will not find it difficult to engage a Dutch person in conversation but be prepared for lots of personal information and frank observation. You might find some questions a little too direct or downright blunt, but remember that they are not meant to offend, it is simply a Dutch person's way of conducting a conversation.

YOUR TURN

Exercise 1

Respond appropriately in the following situations:

1. Someone starts talking to you and asks **hoe heet je?**
2. You want to know the other person's name.
3. Ask him/her whether he/she is from The Netherlands.
4. Next you are asked **waar kom jij vandaan?**
5. Tell your new friend which city you live in.
6. Also say that you are on holiday in The Netherlands.
7. He/she asks **wil je iets drinken?** and you react positively.
8. The last question your friend asks before going off to the bar is, naturally, **wat wil je drinken?**
9. Returning from the bar he/she gives you your drink and says **alsjeblieft.**

Exercise 2

You are staying at a friend's house in Antwerp. Your Belgian friend Peter is in the bathroom when his mother drops by.

1. His mother greets you with **goedemorgen**, *good morning*, and introduces herself. You greet her back and introduce yourself.
2. She asks **waar is Peter?** You tell her he is in the bathroom.
3. Then she asks after Peter's flatmate: **waar is Johanna?** You tell her she is on holiday in England.
4. Peter's mother sits down and you ask whether she would like to drink something.
5. She says **een mineraalwater alsjeblieft**. You get her the drink and hand it to her, saying . . .

Exercise 3

Spelling names: try spelling the following Dutch surnames, listen to the cassettes to check how you have done.

1. Metselaar; 2. Smeltink; 3. Hoogbroek; 4. Kok.

Exercise 4

Ordering drinks.

1. You are in a bar with a friend and you ask whether your friend would like a drink.
2. Ask your friend what he or she would like.
3. You both want beer. You walk up to the bar, greet the barman (it is in the afternoon) and ask for two beers.
4. The barman says **dat is 5 gulden**. You hand over a ten-guilder note.
5. The barman hands you the change saying **alstublieft**, you reply with . . .

Exercise 5

Back to school: adding and subtracting.

Work out the following sums and read out the whole sum in Dutch (+ is pronounced as **plus**, − is pronounced as **min** and = is **is**). Listen to the cassettes and try to imitate the sounds as closely as possible.

$25 + 40 =$
$32 + 64 =$
$87 - 16 =$
$51 + 13 =$
$77 - 22 =$

WORD LIST

de achternaam	last name, surname
het alfabet	alphabet
het appelsap	apple juice
het bier	beer
een biertje	one beer
het café	café/bar/pub
Engeland	England
Londen	London
het mineraalwater	mineral water
moe	tired
Nederland	The Netherlands
de vakantie	holiday
de vriend	(boy)friend
de vriendin	(girl)friend
de wijn	wine

USEFUL EXPRESSIONS

een prettige vakantie!	have a nice holiday!
goedemorgen	good morning
goedemiddag	good afternoon
goedenavond	good evening
ja graag	yes please
kun je dat spellen?	could you spell that?
prettig kennis te maken	pleased to meet you

KEY

Exercise 1

1. Ik heet [your name]; 2. Wat is je naam?; 3. Kom je uit Nederland?; 4. Ik kom uit [your home country]; 5. Ik woon in [the city you live in]; 6. Ik ben op vakantie in Nederland; 7. Ja graag; 8. Een [your favourite drink] graag; 9. Bedankt/dank je wel.

Exercise 2

1. Goedemorgen, ik ben/mijn naam is [your name], prettig kennis te maken; 2. Hij is in de badkamer; 3. Zij is op vakantie in Engeland; 4. Wilt u iets drinken? 5. Alstublieft.

Exercise 4

1. Wil je iets drinken; 2. Wat wil je; 3. Goedemiddag, drie bier alstublieft/graag; 4. alstublieft; 5. dank u wel.

Exercise 5

65; 96; 71; 64; 55

4 In Town

Jane is in Amsterdam and would like to visit the Rijksmuseum. She asks a passer-by for the way.

Jane: Goedemorgen, kunt u me helpen? Weet u waar het Rijksmuseum is?
Good morning, could you help me? Do you know where the Rijksmuseum is?

Passer-by 1: Ja hoor. U gaat hier rechtsaf, voorbij het postkantoor en dan gaat u bij de stoplichten rechtsaf. U neemt de derde straat links en het Rijksmuseum is het oude gebouw aan uw linkerhand.
Yes, certainly. Go straight ahead here, past the post office and then turn right at the traffic lights. Take the

third street on the left and the Rijksmuseum is the old
building on your left.

Jane: Is het ver?
Is it far?

Passer-by 1: Nee hoor, ongeveer tien minuten lopen.
No, about a ten-minute walk.

Jane: Dank u wel.
Thank you.

Half an hour later:

Jane: Pardon meneer, ik ben verdwaald, bent u hier
bekend?
Excuse me sir, I'm lost, do you know the area?

Passer-by 2: Ja hoor, waar wilt u naartoe?
Yes, I do. Where do you want to get to?

Jane: Ik zoek het Rijksmuseum.
I'm looking for the Rijksmuseum.

Passer-by 2: Aha. U neemt de eerste zijstraat links en u loopt
rechtdoor. Dan gaat u een brug over en loopt u
tot de tweede stoplichten. Bij de stoplichten
rechtsaf en het Rijksmuseum is aan het einde van
de lange straat.
*I see. Take the first side street on the left and walk
straight ahead. You cross a bridge and walk up to the
second traffic lights. Turn right at the traffic lights and
the Rijksmuseum is at the end of the long street.*

Jane: Is het ver?
Is it far?

Passer-by 2: Nee, het is heel dichtbij.
No, it is really close.

Jane: Dank u wel meneer.
Thank you, sir.

Passer-by 2: Graag gedaan.
You're welcome.

Half an hour later:

Jane: Pardon, mag ik u iets vragen? Is dit grote gebouw
het Rijksmuseum?

Excuse me, can I ask you something? Is this large building the Rijksmuseum?

Passer-by 3: Nee, dit is het Paleis op de Dam. Ik zal u vertellen waar het Rijksmuseum is. U gaat hier rechtsaf en u loopt rechtdoor tot u bij een oude kerk komt. Dan moet u de weg oversteken en gaat u rechtsaf. U loopt door tot de rotonde. Bij de rotonde linksa en dan ziet u links een oud gebouw aan de overkant van de gracht. Dat is het Rijksmuseum.
No, this is the Royal Palace. I'll tell you where the Rijksmuseum is. Turn right here and walk straight ahead until you reach an old church. Cross the road and turn right. Walk up to the roundabout. Turn left at the roundabout and then you'll see an old building across the canal. That's the Rijksmuseum.

Jane: Is het ver?
Is it far?

Passer-by 3: Nou, ongeveer twintig minuten lopen.
Well, about a 20-minute walk.

Jane: Bedankt.
Thanks.

Passer-by 3: Geen dank.
Not at all.

HOW IT WORKS

ON THE MOVE

The most common way of giving people directions is by starting with **u/je moet** or **u/je gaat**:

je moet linksaf
turn left

u moet rechtdoor
go straight ahead

je gaat rechtsaf
turn right

u gaat rechtdoor
go straight ahead

When referring to a particular turning you use **neemt**:

u neemt de eerst afslag links
take the first turning on the left

je neemt de derde straat rechts
take the third street on the right

Another way of directing people is to use **loopt**:

u loopt rechtdoor	*walk straight ahead*
je loopt voorbij het station	*walk past the station*
u loopt tot de rotonde	*walk as far as the roundabout*
je loopt naar het zebrapad	*walk to the zebra crossing*

Note that word order changes after **dan**:

u gaat hier rechtsaf . . . en dan gaat u rechtsaf
u gaat hier rechtsaf . . . dan moet u de weg oversteken
u loopt tot de rotonde . . . dan ziet u links een oud gebouw

The verb is always the second item in a sentence so if you start your sentence with **dan** the verb must follow it directly.

LINKS OF RECHTS?

Some of the most important directions are also the most basic ones: **rechtdoor**, **links** and **rechts**, which are used like the English *straight ahead*, *left* and *right*. To indicate a left or right turn or the left-hand or right-hand side Dutch uses variations of **links** and **rechts**:

rechtdoor	
links	**rechts**
linksaf	**rechtsaf**
aan de linkerkant	**aan de rechterkant**
aan je/uw linkerhand	**aan je/uw rechterhand**

Linksaf and **rechtsaf** mean *to the left/right* and can be used with **gaat** and **moet** or without a verb.

u gaat linksaf	*go to the left*
je moet rechtsaf	*go to the right*
dan linksaf	*then to the left*

Rechtdoor can also be used with **gaat**, **moet** or without a verb.

je gaat rechtdoor	*go straight ahead*
u moet rechtdoor	*go straight ahead*
rechtsaf en dan rechtdoor	*to the right and then straight ahead*

Aan de linkerkant/rechterkant indicates whether something is on the left or the right.

de kerk is aan de linkerkant
the church is on the left

het museum is aan de rechterkant
the museum is on the right

Aan je/uw linkerhand/rechterhand indicate the same, but refer to your left- or right-hand side.

het postkantoor is aan je linkerhand
the post office is on your left-hand side

u ziet de brug aan uw rechterhand
you will see the bridge on your right-hand side

OUD, LANG, MOOI

When giving directions, people often describe places and buildings. Instead of saying *pass the building on your left* they will *say pass the old building on your left*. Here are some Dutch words that give a description like that:

oud	*old*
lang	*long*
mooi	*beautiful*

The dialogues show that these words are given an **-e** ending when put in front of the word they describe:

het oude gebouw	*the old building*
de lange straat	*the long street*
een oude kerk	*an old church*

However, there is one exception, compare **het oude gebouw** with **een oud gebouw**. When you are using **een** rather than **het**, the **-e** is not added: the *beautiful hotel* is **het mooie hotel**, whereas *a beautiful hotel* is **een mooi hotel**.

There is no need to worry about **de** words, simply always add the **-e**. **De kerk**, for instance, can be described as **de oude kerk** or as **een oude kerk**.

Here are some examples showing the difference between **de** and **het** words:

de oude brug	**een oude brug**
het oude hotel	**een oud hotel**
de mooie kamer	**een mooie kamer**
het mooie huis	**een mooi huis**

EERSTE, TWEEDE, DERDE

Another way of giving a description is by using numbers, for instance by saying a certain street is *the first street on the left*. We find several examples in the dialogue:

de eerste zijstraat links	*the first side street left*
de tweede stoplichten	*the second set of traffic lights*
de derde straat links	*the third street on the left*

eerste	*first*	**zesde**	*sixth*
tweede	*second*	**zevende**	*seventh*
derde	*third*	**achtste**	*eighth*
vierde	*fourth*	**negende**	*ninth*
vijfde	*fifth*	**tiende**	*tenth*

Note that with the exception of **eerste**, **derde** and **achtste** the ordinals, as they are called, are made by simply adding **-de** to the cardinal numbers.

JA HOOR – NEE HOOR

You will have noticed in the dialogues that people often use **ja hoor** or **nee hoor** instead of just **ja** or **nee**. This **hoor** makes the **ja** or **nee** less curt and direct, which encourages the other speaker to continue. The translations of the dialogues show there isn't one single English translation for **hoor** and often it can't be translated at all but don't let this bother you, simply use hoor whenever you can to be as friendly as possible.

ZOEKEN, WONEN, LIGGEN

We're going to have a look at three regular verbs now. All Dutch verbs have a basic form, which is found by taking away the **-en** ending of the whole verb. For **zoeken** this basic form is **zoek**. All verbs use the basic form after **ik**, in this case **ik zoek**. The other forms of regular verbs are made by adding **-t** or **-en** to the basic form.

zoeken	*to be looking for*

singular:
ik zoek	*I am looking for*
jij zoekt	*you are looking for* (informal)
u zoekt	*you are looking for* (formal)
hij/zij/het zoekt	*he/she/it is looking for*

plural:
wij zoeken	*we are looking for*
jullie zoeken	*you are looking for* (informal)
u zoekt	*you are looking for* (formal)
zij zoeken	*they are looking for*

All regular verbs work in exactly the same way. Note that these forms can only be used when talking about 'now'. If you want to talk about the past, for instance, you should use other forms, which will be discussed later.

Now let's look at **wonen** (*to live*), another regular verb:

singular:
ik woon	*I live*
jij woont	*you walk* (informal)
u woont	*you walk* (formal)
hij/zij/het woont	*he/she/it walks*

plural:
wij wonen	*we walk*
jullie wonen	*you walk* (informal)
u woont	*you walk* (formal)
zij wonen	*they walk*

You can see the basic form of **wonen** is not **won**, as you might expect if you simply take away **-en**, but **woon**. This doesn't mean **wonen** is an irregular verb. The **o** is doubled because of the spelling rules explained in chapter one: the o-sound found in **wonen** is spelt with double **o** in a closed syllable such as **woon**. **Wonen** is completely regular but we mustn't forget the spelling rules.

Another spelling rule applies to **liggen**. Because Dutch words cannot end in a double consonant the basic form of **liggen** isn't **ligg** but **lig**.

liggen	*to lie*

singular:

ik lig	*I lie*
jij ligt	*you lie* (informal)
u ligt	*you lie* (formal)
hij/zij/het ligt	*he/she/it lies*

plural:

wij liggen	*we lie*
jullie liggen	*you lie* (informal)
u ligt	*you lie* (formal)
zij liggen	*they lie*

Here are some more regular verbs:

werken (basic form: **werk**)	*to work*
drinken (basic form: **drink**)	*to drink*
lopen (basic form: **loop**)	*to walk*

Note that there are also quite a few irregular verbs, like **zijn**, which we saw in the previous chapter.

NUMBERS 100–1000

In the last chapter we counted up to 100. Let's go now up to 1000.

100	**honderd**	600	**zeshonderd**
200	**tweehonderd**	700	**zevenhonderd**
300	**driehonderd**	800	**achthonderd**
400	**vierhonderd**	900	**negenhonderd**
500	**vijfhonderd**	1000	**duizend**

Combined numbers between 100 and 1000 are made by putting the hundreds in front of the lower numbers, with the hundreds and tens written separately.

150	**honderd vijftig**
490	**vierhonderd negentig**
134	**honderd vierendertig**

HOW TO ...

Ask for directions

pardon, meneer/mevrouw	*excuse me, sir/madam*
mag ik u/je iets vragen?	*may I ask you something?*
kunt u/kun je me helpen?	*can you help me?*
bent u/ben je hier bekend?	*do you know the area?*
ik zoek . . .	*I am looking for . . .*
waar is . . . ?	*where is . . . ?*
weet u/je waar . . . is?	*do you know where . . . is?*

Of course there are many different ways of approaching people in order to ask them for directions. The phrases above can be combined to make up many different variations. However, always remember to be polite, and for that reason it is a good idea to start with **pardon** whatever you are asking and whoever you are approaching.

Pardon, mag ik u iets vragen? Bent u hier bekend? Ik zoek . . .

STREETWISE

The population of The Netherlands is more than 15 million, making it one of the most densely populated countries in the world. The largest concentration of people can be found in the area known as **de Randstad**, an urban area in the west of the country, including the four largest cities: **Amsterdam**, **Den Haag** (*The Hague*), **Rotterdam** and **Utrecht**. These four cities contain some of the country's finest museums, galleries, theatres, tourist attractions and night-life. Although these four are not as big as some world cities, it may still be a good idea to buy a **plattegrond**, *a map*, before starting your explorations.

Amsterdam is the country's capital and houses well-known museums like **het Van Goghmuseum** and **het Rijksmuseum**, **het Koninklijk Concertgebouw en het Concertgebouworkest**, the renowned concert building and its orchestra, **het Anne Frankhuis**, **de grachten**, *canals*, and of course the infamous **de wallen**, the red-light district.

Den Haag is both the royal residence and the seat of government. One of its main attractions are the houses of parliament, known as **het Binnenhof**, a group of buildings the oldest of which, the hall of knights or **de Ridderzaal**, dates back to medieval times. **Den Haag** is also home to the international court of justice, which is housed in **het Vredespaleis**, *the peace palace*.

Rotterdam was extensively bombed during World War II and was rebuilt in sometimes striking architectural styles. The town centre contains some good examples of these, **de kubuswoningen**, which are cube-shaped houses on top of concrete pillars. **Rotterdam** also has one of the largest and busiest ports in the world.

Utrecht is home to **de Dom van Utrecht**, a church with a famous high tower, **de dom**. Large national trade shows are often held at **de jaarbeurshallen** centre, which adjoins the railway station. **Utrecht** is also much loved for the many cafés along its picturesque canals.

YOUR TURN

Exercise 1

Look at the map below. Try to find out which buildings identified by letter (ABCDE) correspond to those named in the following questions, by reading the directions given (from these you can tell whether it is a formal or informal situation). First, formulate a polite request for directions to each place.

1. De bank
   U gaat rechtdoor en neemt de eerste straat links. Dan gaat u rechtsaf en gaat u voorbij de rotonde. De bank is aan uw linkerhand.
2. Het museum
   Je neem de eerste zijstraat links. Dan rechtdoor en aan het einde van de straat rechtsaf. Het museum is aan je linkerhand.
3. Het hotel
   U loopt rechtdoor tot de stoplichten. U neemt de eerste zijstraat links en het hotel is aan uw linkerhand.

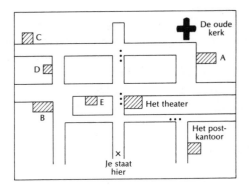

4. Het station
   U gaat rechtdoor en neemt de tweede afslag rechts en de eerste afslag links. Het station is rechts.

5. De supermarkt
   Je gaat rechtdoor, voorbij het theater, tot de tweede stoplichten. Bij de stoplichten linksaf en dan rechtdoor. De supermarkt is aan de rechterkant.

6. De Stolwijkstraat
   Je neemt de eerste zijstraat links. Je loopt rechtdoor en je gaat rechtsaf. De Stolwijkstraat is de eerste straat links.

Exercise 2

Combine the following words with **de/het** and **een**, respectively, to make short descriptive phrases. As always, if you do not know a word, look it up in the word list.

Example: oud, gebouw = het oude gebouw, een oud gebouw.

1. lang, brug
2. oud, museum
3. jong, kind
4. klein, jongen
5. mooi, gebouw
6. zwart, auto

WORD LIST

de afslag	turning
de brug	bridge
dichtbij	close
het gebouw	building
de gracht	canal
jong	young
de kerk	church
klein	small

lang	long/tall
mooi	beautiful
oud	old
het postkantoor	post office
de rotonde	roundabout
het station	station
het stoplicht	traffic lights
de straat	street
de supermarkt	supermarket
het theater	theatre
ver	far
het zebrapad	zebra crossing
de zijstraat	side street
zwart	black

USEFUL EXPRESSIONS

aan de overkant	across/on the other side
bent u/ben je hier bekend?	do you know the area?
ik ben verdwaald	I'm lost
kunt u/kun je me helpen?	can you help me?
mag ik u/je iets vragen?	may I ask you something?

KEY

Exercise 1

1. Pardon meneer/mevrouw, kunt u me helpen? Ik zoek de bank. (D)
2. Pardon, mag ik je iets vragen? Waar is het museum? (B)
3. Pardon, bent u hier bekend? Weet u waar het hotel is? (E)
4. Pardon meneer/mevrouw, ik zoek het station. (A)
5. Pardon, ben je hier bekend? Weet je waar de supermarkt is? (C)
6. Pardon, kun je me helpen? Ik zoek de Stolwijkstraat. (Runs parallel to de Rubenslaan. De supermarkt is in de Rubenslaan.)

Exercise 2

1. de lange brug, een lange brug; 2. het oude museum, een oud museum; 3. het jonge kind, een jong kind; 4. de kleine jongen, een kleine jongen; 5. het mooie gebouw, een mooi gebouw; de zwarte auto, een zwarte auto.

5 By Train and Tram

Jordan and Miriam are going on a day-trip to The Hague. Jordan buys the tickets at the counter, **het loket** (**de lokettiste** is the woman behind the counter).

Lokettiste:	Goedemorgen.
	Good morning.
Jordan:	Goedemorgen, twee retourtjes Den Haag en een strippenkaart, alstublieft.
	Good morning, two returns to The Hague and a 'strippenkaart', please.
Lokettiste:	Dat is vijfenvijftig gulden, alstublieft.
	That's 55 guilders, please.
Jordan:	Hoe laat vertrekt de trein naar Den Haag?
	What time does the train to The Hague leave?
Lokettiste:	Er gaat een sneltrein om kwart voor en kwart over en er gaat een stoptrein elk heel en half uur. U haalt de sneltrein van kwart voor tien nog als u snel bent.
	There is an express train at a quarter to and a quarter

past, and there is a slow train on the hour and half past
the hour. If you're quick, you can still make the express
train at a quarter to ten.

Jordan: Van welk spoor vertrekt de sneltrein?
From which platform does the express train leave?

Lokettiste: Van spoor 4A.
From platform 4A.

Jordan: Dank u wel.
Thank you.

Lokettiste: Geen dank.
Not at all.

Miriam asks a passer-by where the platform is.

Miriam: Pardon meneer, weet u waar perron 4A is?
Excuse me, sir, do you know where platform 4A is?

Passer-by: Ja hoor. Je moet hier rechts en dan rechtdoor tot je
een bord ziet met vier A erop. Dan moet je gewoon
de trap op.
*Yes. Go right here and then go straight ahead until you see
a sign saying 4A. Then simply go up the stairs.*

Miriam: Dank u wel.
Thank you.

There is no train on the platform. Jordan asks someone.

Jordan: Is dit het juiste spoor voor de trein naar Den Haag?
Is this the right platform for the train to The Hague?

Traveller: Ja, maar hij is al vertrokken, u heeft de trein gemist.
Yes, but it has left already, you have missed the train.

Jordan: Verdorie. Dan moeten we wachten. Hoe laat is het?
Damn. We'll have to wait. What time is it?

Traveller: Het is bijna tien voor tien. *It is nearly ten to ten.*

Jordan: Hoe laat gaat de stoptrein?
When does the slow train leave?

Traveller: Over ongeveer tien minuten.
In about ten minutes.

Jordan: Bedankt.
Thanks.

In The Hague Miriam and Jordan catch a tram to the parliament buildings, **het Binnenhof**. They want to know where to stamp their **strippenkaart** so they ask a fellow traveller.

> *Miriam:* Pardon meneer, waar kunnen we afstempelen?
> *Excuse me, sir, where can we stamp our cards?*
>
> *Traveller:* Bij de chauffeur of in een stempelautomaat. Er is een stempelautomaat achterin de tram.
> *With the driver or in a ticket-stamping machine. There's a machine in the back of the tram.*
>
> *Miriam:* Hoeveel strippen moeten we afstempelen?
> *How many strips should we stamp?*
>
> *Traveller:* Waar gaan jullie naartoe?
> *Where are you going?*
>
> *Miriam:* We gaan naar het Binnenhof.
> *We are going to the Binnenhof.*
>
> *Traveller:* Dat is twee zones, dus jullie moeten elk drie strippen afstempelen.
> *That is two zones, so you should stamp three strips each.*
>
> *Miriam:* Weet u waar we moeten uitstappen?
> *Do you know where we should get off?*
>
> *Traveller:* Ja, je moet bij de zesde halte uitstappen, dat is vlakbij het Binnenhof.
> *Yes, you should get off at the sixth stop, that's near the Binnenhof.*

HOW IT WORKS

DE KLOK

Catching trains and trams is one thing, but if you don't know what time they leave you will have a hard time catching them. Here's the Dutch way of telling the time.

het is acht uur	*it's eight o'clock*
het is half acht	*it's half past seven*
het is tien uur	*it's ten o'clock*
het is half tien	*it's half past nine*

For the half hour Dutch uses **half**, like English, but note that the Dutch half hour anticipates the coming hour so **half tien** is not *half past ten* but *half past nine*.

For the other times, we can divide the clock into two parts, top and bottom.

The top half of the clock refers to the hour in the same way as English:

het is tien voor zes	*it's ten to six*
het is vijf over zes	*it's five past six*
het is kwart voor drie	*it's a quarter to three*
het is kwart over elf	*it's a quarter past eleven*

The bottom half of the clock takes the half hour as its point of reference. Note again that the half hour looks forward to the coming hour:

het is tien voor half acht	*it's twenty past seven*
het is vijf voor half zeven	*it's twenty-five past six*
het is vijf over half twee	*it's twenty-five to two*
het is tien over half vijf	*it's twenty to five*

Dutch describes the time of day to indicate *a.m.* or *p.m.*: **acht uur 's ochtends**, *eight o'clock* (in the morning); **tien uur 's avonds**, *ten o'clock* (at night).

am:	**'s nachts**	*at night*
	's ochtends/'s morgens	*in the morning*
pm:	**'s middags**	*in the afternoon*
	's avonds	*in the evening*
half negen 's morgens		*8.30 a.m.*
tien voor vier 's middags		*3.50 p.m.*
vijf over half acht 's avonds		*7.35 p.m.*
kwart over twee 's nachts		*2.15 a.m.*

In timetables like those in railway stations the 24-hour clock will often be used. The 24-hour clock operates in the same way as in English.

22.45	=	**tweeëntwintig uur vijfenveertig**
13.10	=	**dertien uur tien**

Here are some frequently used measures of time:

we zijn tien <u>seconden</u> te laat
we're ten seconds late

de trein vertrekt over tien <u>minuten</u>
the train leaves in ten minutes

de trein gaat over drie <u>kwartier</u>
the train leaves in three quarters of an hour

we moeten <u>een half uur</u> wachten
we have to wait half an hour

de trein heeft twee <u>uur</u> vertraging
the train has been delayed for two hours

Note that **kwartier** and **uur** are always used in the singular.

MOETEN AND KUNNEN

Have a look at the following sentences:

we moeten wachten	*we have to wait*
je kunt hier afstempelen	*you can stamp here*

These sentences illustrate that, whenever **moeten** and **kunnen** are used with another verb, this second verb (a) always comes at the very end of the sentence, and (b) is always an infinitive, i.e. the whole verb with its **-en** ending.

Here are the two verbs in full.

moeten *have to/must*	**kunnen** *can/be possible*
singular:	
ik moet	**ik kan**
jij moet	**jij kunt/kan**
u moet	**u kunt/kan**
hij/zij/het moet	**hij/zij/het kan**
plural:	
wij moeten	**wij kunnen**
jullie moeten	**jullie kunnen**
u moet	**u kunt/kan**
zij moeten	**zij kunnen**

The two forms of **kunnen** for **jij** and **u**, **kunt/kan**, mean exactly the same and can be interchanged freely.

Note that **moeten** is regular but that, since Dutch words cannot end in a double consonant, the forms for **jij/u/hij/zij/het** end in only one **-t** and not in two.

GAAN AND HEBBEN

Here are two more useful verbs:

gaan *to go*	**hebben** *to have*
singular:	
ik ga	**ik heb**
jij gaat	**jij hebt**
u gaat	**u hebt/heeft**
hij/zij/het gaat	**hij/zij/het heeft**
plural:	
wij gaan	**wij hebben**
jullie gaan	**jullie hebben**
u hebt/heeft	**u hebt/heeft**
zij hebben	**zij hebben**

The two forms of **hebben** for **u**, **hebt** and **heeft**, can be interchanged freely.

Here are some examples of these two verbs at work:

hoe laat gaat de trein?	*what time does the train leave?*
waar gaan jullie naartoe?	*where are you going?*
we gaan naar Den Haag	*we're going to The Hague*
heb je een strippenkaart?	*do you have a 'strippenkaart'?*
we hebben een strippenkaart	*we have a 'strippenkaart'*

WHERE ARE YOU GOING?

When asking someone *where are you going?* Dutch uses **waar ... naartoe**. Addressing one person you would ask:

waar ga je naartoe? or **waar gaat u naartoe?**

Speaking to more than one person you would ask:

waar gaan jullie naartoe? or **waar gaat u naartoe?**

The answer to such questions is made with **naar**:

ik ga naar Arnhem	*I'm going to Arnhem*
we gaan naar Epe	*we're going to Epe*

GAAT AND VERTREKT

For information about train departures both **gaat** and **vertrekt**, *departs/leaves,* can be used.

hoe laat gaat de trein?	*what time does the train leave?*
van welk spoor vertrekt de trein?	*from which platform does the train depart?*
de trein gaat over een kwartier	*the train will leave in a quarter of an hour*

WHICH BUS OR TRAM?

When catching a bus or tram you will want to find out which one you're supposed to catch and where to find it. Here's how to ask which bus or tram is going your way:

welke bus gaat naar Leiden?	*which bus goes to Leiden?*
welke tram gaat naar het Concertgebouw?	*which tram goes to the Concertgebouw?*

The answer may be:

bus negentien	*bus number nineteen,* or
tram een of drie	*tram number one or three*

Note that **welke** becomes **welk** in front of **het**-words (see chapter four):

welk hotel is dat?	*which hotel is that?*

When asking where to find a bus or tram you should use **staat** (literally *'stands'*):

waar staat de bus naar Haarlem?	*where can I find the bus to Haarlem?*
waar staat tram drie?	*where can I find tram number three?*

HOW TO ...

Ask the time

There are several ways of asking the time, but the most straightforward is:

hoe laat is het? *what time is it?*

When asking a stranger you may want to be a little more polite and elaborate:

weet u hoe laat het is? *do you know the time?*
weet je hoe laat het is? *do you know the time?*

As we saw in the last chapter, there are various ways of making your request even more polite. Here is an example:

Pardon mevrouw, mag ik u iets vragen? Weet u hoe laat het is?
Excuse me, madam, can I ask you something? Do you know the time?

Buy tickets

You can read more about the different types of tickets for public transport in <u>Streetwise</u> below. Here we'll take a look at the various ways of asking for a ticket. Note the similarities with ordering a drink, which we saw in chapter 3.

een enkeltje Enschede, alstublieft/alsjeblieft
a single to Enschede, please

twee enkeltjes Brugge, graag
two single tickets to Brugge, please

mag ik een retour Den Helder, alstublieft/alsjeblieft?
may I have a return Den Helder, please?

As we saw with buying drinks, the most important phrases for rounding off an exchange politely are:

alstublieft/alsjeblieft for handing over the money, and **dank u wel/dank je wel** when receiving the ticket.

STREETWISE

The Netherlands has an extensive public transport network. **Trein- en busdiensten**, *train and bus services*, are in operation throughout the country. In the four largest cities, Amsterdam, Den Haag, Rotterdam and Utrecht, there are also **trams** and in addition Amsterdam and Rotterdam operate an underground system, **de metro**.

Train tickets, **een enkeltje/een enkele reis**, *a single*, or **een retourtje**, *a return*, can be bought at **het station**, *the train station*, which can be found in a central location in most medium-sized and large towns and usually adjoins **het busstation**, *the bus station*. Towns with more than one train station have one main station, **het centraal station**. Big yellow timetables indicate **de vertrektijden**, *departure times*, and whether the train will be **een stoptrein**, *a slow train*, or **een sneltrein** or **intercity**, *a fast train*. Big signs on the *platform*, **het perron** or **het spoor**, give up-to-date information about departure times and possible *delays*, **vertragingen**.

Journeys by bus, tram or metro are paid for by **strippenkaart**, a card with a number of strips which are to be *stamped*, **afstempelen**, at the start of each journey. The number of strips to be stamped depends on the number of **zones** you travel in; one strip per zone plus one zone extra per journey. The strips can be stamped by travellers themselves in special machines on the bus or tram or at **het (metro)station**, or by the driver or conductor on the bus or tram. **Strippenkaarten** can be bought at train or bus stations, the post office or in newsagents. They can also be bought from drivers on buses and trams, but this is more expensive.

Most services close down at some point between midnight and one a.m.. However, *night bus* services, **de nachtbus**, run in the larger cities and some *night train* services, **de nachttrein**, run between them.

YOUR TURN

Exercise 1

Complete the following dialogue:

You're going to visit a friend in Maastricht by train. At the station you walk up to the counter and ask for a return to Maastricht (1). You also ask what time the train leaves (2). The answer is **de trein gaat om kwart voor elf**. You ask from which platform (3). You're told **de trein gaat van spoor 7B**. You hand over the money, get the ticket and thank the person behind the counter (4). You walk to the platform and ask someone else the time (5). The person says **het is vijf over half elf** and then asks you **hoe laat gaat de trein?** Reply that the train will leave in ten minutes (6).

Exercise 2

Hoe laat is het? Tell the time from the six clocks below in Dutch.

1. Hoe laat is het?   2. Hoe laat is het?   3. Hoe laat is het?

4. Hoe laat is het?   5. Hoe laat is het?   6. Hoe laat is het?

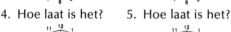

Exercise 3

Fill in an appropriate form of **moeten, kunnen, gaan** or **hebben**.

1. We ... drie strippen afstempelen.
2. Ik ... al een kaartje.
3. Je ... op het station een kaartje kopen.
4. ... u naar Den Bosch met de trein?
5. Jullie ... om kwart over acht op het station zijn.
6. Monica ... een half uur op de trein wachten.
7. ... je een gulden voor me?
8. We ... de strippenkaart in de stempelautomaat afstempelen.
9. Ze ... met de tram naar het museum.
10. George ... geen strippenkaart voor de bus.

WORD LIST

achterin	in the back
afstempelen	to stamp
bijna	nearly/almost
het bord	sign
de bus	bus
de chauffeur	driver
de enkele reis	single ticket/journey
het enkeltje	single ticket
de halte	the stop (public transport)
kopen	to buy
het loket	counter
de lokettist(e)	man (woman) behind counter
de metro	the underground
naar	to
het perron	platform
het retour	return ticket
het retourtje	return ticket
de sneltrein	express train
het spoor	platform
de stempelautomaat	stamping machine (in buses/trams)
de stoptrein	slow train
de strippenkaart	'strippenkaart' (ticket for bus/tram/tube)
de tram	tram
de trap	stairs
uitstappen	to get off
vlakbij	close (by)
wachten	to wait
wachten op	to wait for
de zone	zone

USEFUL EXPRESSIONS

de trein is vertrokken	the train has left
hoe laat . . .?	what time . . .?
op het station	at the station
u heeft de trein gemist	you have missed the train

KEY

Exercise 1

1. Een retour Maastricht alstublieft;   2. Hoe laat vertrekt/gaat de trein?;   3. Van welk spoor/perron gaat/vertrekt de trein?
4. Bedankt/Dank u wel;   5. Pardon, weet u hoe laat het is?   6. De trein gaat over tien minuten.

Exercise 2

1. Het is half negen;   2. Het is kwart voor twee;   3. Het is tien over half vier;   4. Het is acht uur;   5. Het is vijf voor half twaalf;   6. Het is vijf over drie.

Exercise 3

1. moeten;   2. heb;   3. kunt/kan;   4. gaat;   5. moeten;   6. moet;
7. heb;   8. kunnen;   9. gaan; 10. heeft.

6 At the Post Office

POSTKANTOOR

Julie and Remco want to have a coffee in town but Julie has run out of money and needs to change some more English pounds.

Julie: Ik heb geen geld meer, ik moet geld wisselen.
I have no money left, I'll have to change some money.

Remco: Is je geld nu al op?
You've run out of money already?

Julie: Ja, ik heb gisteren te veel gekocht.
Yes, I bought too much yesterday.

Remco: Waar ben je geweest?
Where did you go?

Julie: Ik ben naar Den Haag geweest.
I went to the Hague.

Remco: Ben je ook naar Scheveningen geweest?
Did you also go to Scheveningen?

Julie: Nee, ik ben niet naar Scheveningen geweest. Ik heb het Binnenhof gezien en ik heb gewinkeld. Ik heb veel souveniers gekocht.

> *No, I didn't go to Scheveningen. I saw the Binnenhof and
> I went shopping. I bought a lot of souvenirs.*

Remco: En nu is je geld op.
And now you've run out of money.

Julie: Precies. Waar kan ik geld wisselen?
Exactly. Where can I change some money?

Remco: Bij het postkantoor of een bank. Laten we maar
naar het postkantoor gaan, dat is dichtbij.
*At the post office or a bank. Let's go to the post office,
that's close by.*

Julie: Okee.
OK.

(••) Julie goes into the post office while Remco waits outside.

Julie: Ik wil graag Engels geld wisselen.
I would like to change some English money, please.

Lokettist 1: Dat kan niet bij dit loket, u moet naar loket zeven.
*That's not possible at this counter, you will have to go to
counter seven.*

Julie: Dank u.
Thank you.

(••)

Julie: Ik wil graag Engels geld wisselen.
I would like to change some English money, please.

Lokettist 2: Dat kan. Hoeveel geld wilt u wisselen?
Certainly. How much would you like to change?

Julie: Ik wil graag vijftig Engelse ponden in Nederlandse
guldens.
*I would like fifty English pounds in Dutch guilders,
please.*

Lokettist 2: Prima. Dan krijgt u honderd achtentwintig gulden
vijftig.
*Right. That will give you a hundred and twenty-eight
guilders and fifty cents.*

Julie: Heeft u het klein?
Could I have it in small change, please?

Lokettist 2: Natuurlijk. Een briefje van vijftig, twee briefjes van
vijfentwintig, een briefje van tien, twee vijfjes, drie
guldens en twee kwartjes.

Of course. One fifty-guilder note, two twenty-five-guilder notes, one ten-guilder note, two five-guilder notes, three guilders and two 25 cent coins.

Julie: Dank u. Verkoopt u ook postzegels?

Thank you. Do you also sell stamps?

Lokettist 2: Jazeker.

Certainly.

Julie: Dan wil ik twee postzegels van zestig en een van zeventig, alstublieft.

Then I'd like two sixty-cent stamps and one seventy cent stamp please.

Lokettist 2: Prima, dat is een gulden negentig.

Very well, that's one guilder and ninety cents.

[*She pays with a 25 guilder note*].

Julie: Alstublieft.

There you are.

Lokettist 2: Heeft u het klein?

Have you anything smaller?

Outside Julie meets up with Remco again.

Remco: Heb je het geld gewisseld?

Have you changed the money?

Julie: Ja, ik heb vijftig pond gewisseld en ik heb ook postzegels gekocht.

Yes, I have changed fifty pounds and I've bought some stamps as well.

Remco: Mooi, zullen we nu een kopje koffie drinken?

Good, shall we have a coffee now?

Julie: Ja, goed. Is café Van Gogh open?

Yes, all right. Is Van Gogh café open?

Remco: Nee, ik denk het niet.

No, I don't think so.

Julie: Zullen we dan naar café Rembrandt gaan?

Shall we go to Rembrandt café then?

Remco: Okee. Betaal jij?

OK. Are you paying?

HOW IT WORKS

TALKING ABOUT THE PAST

Several times in the dialogue Remco and Julie talk about
things that happened in the past. In Dutch there is one
particular formula which is generally used when talking about
the past. In the following examples from the text, the parts of
this formula are underlined.

ik heb gisteren te veel gekocht
I bought too much yesterday

ik ben naar Den Haag geweest
I have been to The Hague

To talk about the past in Dutch you need the following: a
form of **zijn** or **hebben** and a special form of the verb that
describes what you did in the past.

The correct form of **zijn/hebben** will depend on the subject of
the sentence (**ik ben** but **wij zijn**, for instance; see chapters 3
and 5 where these verbs forms are given in full). It comes
second in the sentence with the special past form placed at
the very end of the sentence.

This special past form of the verb is called a 'past participle'
and usually starts with **ge-**, like **gekocht** and **geweest** in our
examples above. The past participle always remains the same.
More details about how the past participle is made will be
given in the next chapter.

WHEN TO USE 'ZIJN' AND WHEN TO USE 'HEBBEN'

Most verbs use a form of **hebben** when talking about the past.

ik heb een boek gekocht	*I have bought a book*
zij heeft gewinkeld	*she has been shopping*

However, a number of frequently used verbs employ **zijn**.
These verbs generally indicate a change of place, for instance:

hij is naar Den Haag geweest *he has been to The Hague*

we zijn met de bus gekomen   *we have come by bus*
ik ben naar huis gegaan   *I went home*

Here are some more useful verbs that are used with a form of **zijn** to talk about the past (their past participles are given in brackets):

blijven (gebleven)   **we zijn thuis gebleven**
to stay   *we stayed at home*

beginnen (begonnen)   **het feest is al begonnen**
to begin/start   *the party has started already*

stoppen (gestopt)   **Jan is met roken gestopt**
to stop/give up   *Jan has given up smoking*

worden (geworden)   **Bella is tandarts geworden**
to become   *Bella has become a dentist*

vallen (gevallen)   **Bas is op zijn knie gevallen**
to fall   *Bas has fallen on his knee*

You may have noticed that these verbs describe a change of state, rather than place.

GEEN AND NIET

In chapter 2 we saw that **geen** means *not any* and that it often replaces **een**.

ik heb een strippenkaart   **ik heb geen strippenkaart**

Geen is also used with things that can't be counted like **suiker** (*sugar*), **geld** (*money*) and **tijd** (*time*):

ik heb geen suiker in huis   *I have no sugar in the house*
we hebben geen geld   *we have no money*
het spijt me, geen tijd!   *sorry, no time!*

In all other cases Dutch uses **niet** to express not:

ik weet het niet   *I don't know*
ik zie Juliet niet   *I can't see Juliet*
zie je Michel niet?   *can't you see Michel?*

Niet doesn't always appear in the same position. Often **niet** comes at the end of the sentence as in the examples above.

However, **niet** always precedes words like **naar** *to*, **bij** *at*, **in** *in*, **met** *with*:

ik ben niet naar	*I haven't been to*
Scheveningen geweest	*Scheveningen*
dat kan niet bij dit loket	*that's not possible at this counter*
ik wil niet met de trein	*I don't want to go by train*

Niet also precedes descriptive words that give more information about another word (including verbs). Some examples (the descriptive words are underlined):

het café is niet <u>open</u>	*the café isn't open*
het hotel is niet <u>ver</u>	*the hotel isn't far*
de film is niet <u>goed</u>	*the film isn't good*

WILLEN

In the previous chapter we saw that if **moeten** and **kunnen** occur with another verb, this second verb is an infinitive, i.e. the whole verb, and is placed at the end of the sentence. As you can see from the examples, the same is true of **willen**, *to want*:

ik wil geld wisselen	*I want to change money*
Remco en Julie willen	*Remco and Julie want to*
koffie drinken	*drink coffee*

singular
ik wil	*I want*
jij wilt	*you want* (informal)
u wilt	*you want* (formal)
hij/zij/het wil	*he/she/it wants*

plural
wij willen	*we want*
jullie willen	*you want* (informal)
u wilt	*you want* (formal)
zij willen	*they want*

As the following examples show, **moeten**, **kunnen** and **willen** can also be used on their own (often a verb like *do*, *go* or *have* is implied):

u moet naar loket zeven	*you have to go to counter seven*
ik moet naar huis	*I have (to go) home*
dat kan	*that's possible (= that can be done . . .)*
ik wil koffie	*I would like (to have) coffee*

HOW TO ...

Make suggestions

At several points in the dialogue suggestions are made:
laten we naar het postkantoor gaan
let's go to the post office

zullen we naar café Rembrandt gaan?
shall we go to café Rembrandt?

Laten we and **zullen we?** operate in the same way as the English *let's* and *shall we?* except that in Dutch the second verb is placed at the very end of the sentence.

Here are some more examples:

laten we naar Hoorn gaan	*let's go to Hoorn*
zullen we uit eten gaan?	*shall we go out for dinner?*
laten we René vragen	*let's ask René*
zullen we tv kijken?	*shall we watch tv?*

STREETWISE

The Dutch currency is **de gulden**, *guilder*, which is divided into **100 cent**. **De munten**, *coins*, come in different sizes and are either a silver or a copper colour. **De briefjes**, *notes*, are all the same size but come in many different, extremely bright colours. Note that some of the coins and notes have special names which are used often in everyday language. (Also note that **cent** and **gulden** are always singular.)

de munten *the coins*	**de briefjes** *the notes*
5 cent (de stuiver)	10 gulden (het tientje)
10 cent (het dubbeltje)	25 gulden
25 cent (het kwartje)	50 gulden
1 gulden (de gulden)	100 gulden

2$\frac{1}{2}$ gulden (de rijksdaalder)   250 gulden
5 gulden   1000 gulden

In The Netherlands you can change foreign currency and cash traveller's cheques at **de bank**, *the bank,* **het postkantoor**, *the post-office,* and **het grenswisselkantoor**, special *bureaux de change* that can be found at most train stations and at **de grens**, *the border*. Banks and post-offices close in the late afternoon, usually between four and five p.m., but **het grenswisselkantoor** normally stays open later.

A large number of cash-dispensing machines, called **de giromaat** or **de geldautomaat**, can be found throughout the country. Credit cards are now generally accepted although it's still best to check before entering shops and restaurants in particular. An increasing number of shops have now also introduced **pinnen**, paying by using your bank card's PIN number; all you have to do is run your card through a machine and enter your PIN number, **de pincode**.

Postzegels, *stamps,* can be bought at the post-office or from newsagents. Red **brievenbussen**, *post-boxes,* can be found in most main streets. They have two slots: one labelled **streekpost** for local mail and one labelled **overige bestemmingen** for all other mail.

YOUR TURN

Exercise 1

The following sentences deal with things in the past. Fill in the gaps with the appropriate form of **zijn** or **hebben** and the past participle of the verb in brackets (new past participles are given).

1. Gisteren . . . ik naar Leeuwarden . . . (zijn).
2. Pieter . . . te veel wijn . . . (drinken/gedronken).
3. We . . . voor iedereen een cadeau . . . (kopen).
4. . . . jullie de hele dag thuis . . . (blijven)?
5. De wedstrijd . . . om half twee . . . (beginnen).
6. . . . Jannie en Henk met de bus of met de trein . . . (komen)?
7. Ik . . . in het nieuwe restaurant . . . (eten/gegeten).
8. Wilma . . . met haar moeder in de stad . . . (winkelen).

Exercise 2

Fill in **geen** or **niet**.

1. Jolanda wil . . . koffie, ze wil thee.
2. We gaan morgen . . . naar Brugge.
3. Het spijt me, het restaurant is vandaag . . . open.
4. Jan en Hilde zijn . . . met de auto gekomen, ze hebben . . . auto.
5. Hebben jullie . . . auto?
6. Zie je de mooie kerk . . . ?
7. Michael heeft . . . strippenkaart.
8. De wasmachine doet het . . .

Exercise 3

Say the following amounts out loud. Then listen to the cassette to check how you are doing.

1. Nfl 12,50
2. Nfl 25,-
3. Nfl 55,35
4. Nfl 5,75
5. Nfl 7,50
6. Nfl 108,-
7. Nfl 36,20
8. Nfl 8,95

Exercise 4

Fill in **zullen**, **laten** or an appropriate form of **willen**, **moeten** or **kunnen**.

1. Ik . . . koffie, . . . jullie ook koffie?
2. We . . . naar de bank want ik . . . geld wisselen.
3. . . . we naar het theater gaan?
4. . . . jullie kaartjes voor het theater kopen?
5. Je . . . twee strippen afstempelen in de tram.
6. . . . we naar het café gaan, ik . . . iets drinken.
7. Je . . . op het postkantoor strippenkaarten kopen.
8. Jannie en Roger . . . . graag Frans eten.

WORD LIST

de auto	car
betalen	to pay
het boek	book
het briefje	note
het cadeau	present/gift

Den Haag	The Hague
Engels	English
Frans	French
het geld	money
gisteren	yesterday
kopen	to buy
het kopje koffie	cup of coffee
het kwartje	25 cent coin
morgen	tomorrow
Nederlands	Dutch
nieuw	new
het pond	pound
de postzegel	stamp
precies	exactly
het restaurant	restaurant
de suiker	sugar
de televisie	television
te veel	too much
de tijd	time
tv kijken	to watch tv
uit eten gaan	to go out for dinner
vandaag	today
verkopen	to sell
de wasmachine	washing machine
de wedstrijd	match/game
winkelen	to shop
wisselen	to change (items, money, etc.)

USEFUL EXPRESSIONS

in huis	in the house
mijn geld is op	I've run out of money

KEY

Exercise 1

1. ben/geweest; 2. heeft/gedronken; 3. hebben/gekocht;
4. zijn/gebleven; 5. is/begonnen; 6. zijn/gekomen;
7. heb/gegeten; 8. heeft/gewinkeld.

Exercise 2

1. geen; 2. niet; 3. niet; 4. niet/geen; 5. geen; 6. niet; 7. geen;
8. niet.

Exercise 4

1. wil/willen; 2. moeten/wil or moet; 3. zullen; 4. kunnen;
5. moet; 6. laten/wil; 7. kan or kunt; 8. willen.

7 In a Restaurant

Louise is going out for dinner with a Dutch friend, Henk. Louise and Henk have just met up in a bar, and are now trying to decide on a restaurant.

Henk: Waar heb je trek in?
What do you feel like eating?

Louise: Ik weet het niet. Welk restaurant raad je aan?
I don't know. What restaurant do you recommend?

Henk: Lieve hemel, dat is moeilijk. Er zijn zo veel restaurants. We kunnen Italiaans eten of Mexicaans of Turks of Frans, of we kunnen naar de Griek, of ... Zeg het maar.
Goodness, that's difficult. There are so many restaurants. We can eat Italian or Mexican, Turkish or French, or we can go Greek, or ... You decide.

Louise: Het klinkt allemaal erg lekker, maar is er niet een
Hollands restaurant in de buurt?
*It all sounds delicious, but isn't there a Dutch
restaurant in the area?*

Henk: Hollands? Dat is niet makkelijk. Er zijn niet zo
veel echte Hollandse restaurants. Maar wacht
even, er is een visrestaurant vlak om de hoek.
Zullen we daar naartoe gaan?
*Dutch? That isn't easy. There aren't that many true
Dutch restaurants. But wait, there is a fish restaurant
just around the corner. Shall we go there?*

Louise: Ja, lekker. Vis!
Yes, lovely. Fish!

In the fish restaurant one of the waiters, **de ober**, approaches
Louise and Henk.

Ober: Goedenavond.
Good evening.

Henk: Goedenavond. Heeft u een tafel voor twee?
Good evening. Would you have a table for two?

Ober: Heeft u gereserveerd?
Did you make a reservation?

Henk: Nee, we hebben niet gereserveerd.
No, we didn't.

Ober: Dan moet u ongeveer tien minuten wachten.
Then you'll have to wait about ten minutes.

Henk: Dat is prima.
That's all right.

At the table, **aan tafel**.

Ober: Wilt u iets drinken?
Would you like a drink?

Louise: Zullen we een fles wijn nemen?
Shall we have a bottle of wine?

Henk: Ja goed. Een fles witte huiswijn, graag. En de
kaart, alstublieft.
*Yes, all right. A bottle of house white, please. And the
menu, please.*

Louise: Weet je al wat je neemt?
Have you decided what to have yet?

69

Henk: Als voorgerecht neem ik groentesoep. Wat neem jij?
I'm having the vegetable soup as a starter. What'll you have?

Louise: Ik heb liever gevulde champignons vooraf.
I'd prefer stuffed mushrooms to start.

Henk: En als hoodgerecht?
And for the main course?

Louise: Hm, de zalm klinkt lekker, maar ik houd ook erg van mosselen.
Well, the salmon sounds nice, but I also love mussels.

Henk: O nee, mosselen lust ik niet. Zalm vind ik wel lekker en tong ook.
Oh no, I don't like mussels. I do like salmon, and sole as well, though.

Ober: Heeft u een keuze gemaakt?
Are you ready to order?

Louise: Ja, ik wil de gevulde champignons als voorgerecht en de gebakken zalm als hoofdgerecht.
Yes, I'd like the stuffed mushrooms as a starter and the fried salmon as a main course.

Henk: En voor mij groentesoep vooraf en daarna tongfilet, alstublieft.
And for me, vegetable soup to start and then filet of sole, please.

Ober: Wilt u friet of aardappels bij de vis?
Would you like french fries or potatoes with the fish?

Louise: Aardappels, graag.
Potatoes, please.

Henk: Voor mij ook, alstublieft.
For me as well, please.

Ober: En welke groentes wilt u?
And which vegetables would you like?

Louise: Hmm, broccoli en worteltjes, alstublieft.
Hmm, broccoli and carrots, please.

Henk: Ik heb liever bloemkool.
I would prefer cauliflower.

The waiter arrives with the food.

> Ober: Alstublieft, de groentesoep en de champignons.
> Eet u smakelijk.
> *There you are, the vegetable soup and the mushrooms.*
> *Enjoy your meal.*
> Henk: Dank u.
> *Thank you.*
> Henk/Louise: Eet smakelijk.
> *Enjoy your meal.*

After the meal.

> Ober: Heeft het gesmaakt?
> *Did you enjoy your meal?*
> Louise: O ja, het was heerlijk.
> *Oh yes, it was delicious.*
> Henk: De tong was ook erg lekker, dank u.
> *The sole was very nice as well, thank you.*
> Ober: Wilt u een nagerecht?
> *Would you like a dessert?*
> Louise: Nee, dank u. Voor mij alleen koffie, graag.
> *No thank you. Just coffee for me, please.*
> Henk: Voor mij hetzelfde, alstublieft.
> *The same for me, please.*

HOW IT WORKS

PAST PARTICIPLES

Heeft u gereserveerd?   *Did you make a reservation?*

From the previous chapter we know that **gereserveerd** is a past participle, a special form of the verb used to talk about the past. In this chapter we will have a look at how past participles are made.

Firstly, consider some past participles you have already learnt:

verb	past participle
winkelen	**gewinkeld**
reserveren	**gereserveerd**
stoppen	**gestopt**

A past participle starts with **ge-** and ends in a **-d** or **-t**. The middle part of a past participle is made up of the basic form of the verb (discussed in chapter 4), which can usually be found by taking away the **-en** ending of the verb.

Here's the formula:

ge + basic form + **t/d**

Our examples illustrate this rule perfectly. They start with **ge-**, followed by the basic forms **winkel**, **reserveer** and **stop** (remember to apply the spelling rules) and end in a **-d** or **-t**. A simple rule tells you whether to add a **-d** or **-t**: a **-t** is added to basic forms ending in **p**, **t**, **k**, **s**, **f** or **ch**, and a **-d** is added to all other basic forms.

Here are some more past participles:

verb (infinitive)	basic form	past part.	
hopen	**hoop**	**gehoopt**	*to hope*
koken	**kook**	**gekookt**	*to cook*
bouwen	**bouw**	**gebouwd**	*to build*
bellen	**bel**	**gebeld**	*to ring*
horen	**hoor**	**gehoord**	*to hear*

Verbs that form their past participle according to these rules are called 'weak verbs'. There is also another group of verbs in Dutch, whose past participles often do not follow any rules at all. The best thing to do is simply memorize these past participles.

We have already seen several examples of these verbs. The past participle of **zijn**, for instance, is **geweest**, and the past participle of **kopen** is **gekocht**. Here are some more past participles that have to be learnt by heart:

verb	past participle	
lezen	**gelezen**	*to read*
vertrekken	**vertrokken**	*to leave*
komen	**gekomen**	*to come*
denken	**gedacht**	*to think*
zien	**gezien**	*to see*
doen	**gedaan**	*to do*

PAST PARTICIPLES AND NIET

In the previous chapter, we saw that **niet** often appears at the end of a sentence as in:

mosselen lust ik niet   *I don't like mussels*

However, we also saw that the past participle is placed at the end of a sentence:

heeft u gereserveerd?   *have you made a reservation?*

What do you do if you have a sentence with both **niet** and a past participle? You say:

we hebben niet gereserveerd
we haven't made a reservation

As you can see, it is the past participle which is placed at the very end of a sentence.

Here are some more examples:

ik heb het boek niet gelezen
I haven't read the book

Jan heeft de film niet gezien
Jan hasn't seen the film

we zijn niet op vakantie geweest
we haven't been on holiday

SEPARABLE VERBS

We <u>gaan</u> vanavond <u>uit</u>	*We're going out tonight*
<u>Raad</u> je het Griekse restaurant <u>aan</u>?	*Do you recommend the Greek restaurant?*
Wanneer <u>komt</u> Jolanda <u>aan</u>?	*When does Jolanda arrive?*

In Dutch there is a group of verbs consisting of two parts that are sometimes separated: an ordinary verb and a small word put in front of this verb, a prefix. These verbs are predictably called *separable verbs*.

The infinitives of separable verbs are written as one word (the prefixes are printed in italics here):

*uit*gaan	*to go out*
*aan*raden	*to recommend*
*aan*komen	*to arrive*

When a separable verb is used in a sentence the two parts of the verb are separated: the main part of the verb is the second item in the sentence and the prefix is placed at the very end of the sentence:

opbellen	*to call* (telephone)
Marcel <u>belt</u> zijn moeder <u>op</u>	*Marcel calls his mother*

afmaken	*to finish*
ik <u>maak</u> de brief morgen <u>af</u>	*I'll finish the letter tomorrow*

When making the past participle of a separable verb, you insert **ge** between the prefix and the verb:

Marcel heeft zijn moeder vanmorgen opgebeld
Marcel called his mother this morning

ik heb de brief gisteren afgemaakt
I finished the letter yesterday

Here are some more past participles of separable verbs:

separable verb	past participle	
uitgaan	**uitgegaan**	*go out*
aanraden	**aangeraden**	*recommend*
aankomen	**aangekomen**	*arrive*

Note that for *to phone* both **bellen** and **opbellen** can be used.

WORD ORDER

Have a look at the following sentences:

ik neem soep als voorgerecht
I'm having soup as a starter

als voorgerecht neem ik soep
I'm having soup as a starter

In the second sentence **als voorgerecht** has moved to the front of the sentence. In Dutch it is possible to place most kinds of information at the beginning of the sentence, as you can see in the following examples:

morgen ga ik naar de film
I'm going to the cinema tomorrow

bij het nagerecht nemen we koffie
we'll have coffee with dessert

Note, however, that the verb always has to be the second item in the sentence (we saw this in chapter 4). This means that if another word or word group is placed at the beginning of the sentence in first position the verb has to come straight after it in second position.

Here are two more examples with the word or word group in position one, *in italics*, and the verb in second position, underlined:

in de tram <u>moet</u> **je een strippenkaart afstempelen**
in the tram you have to stamp a 'strippenkaart'

dan <u>moet</u> **u tien minuten wachten**
then you'll have to wait ten minutes

THE DUTCH CONNECTION (I)

We have already seen several ways of linking sentences:

ik wil soep vooraf <u>en</u> vis als hoofdgerecht
I would like soup to start and fish as a main course

we kunnen Italiaans eten <u>of</u> we kunnen naar de Griek
we can eat Italian or we can go Greek

de zalm klinkt lekker <u>maar</u> ik houd ook van vlees
the salmon sounds nice but I also like meat

Here are two more ways of linking words:

ik moet geld wisselen <u>want</u> ik ben blut
I need to change money because I'm broke

ik ben blut <u>dus</u> ik moet geld wisselen
I'm broke so I need to change money

WEL OF NIET?

Wel is the opposite of **niet** and is used for contrast after something negative has been said:

Mosselen vind ik vies. Zalm vind ik wel lekker.
I hate mussels. I do like salmon.

Jolanda gaat niet uit. Irene en Sharon gaan wel uit.
Jolanda is not going out. Irene and Sharon are going out.

HOW TO ...

Make your preferences known

There are lots of different ways of referring to your personal likes and dislikes. If you like or love something or someone you can use **houden van**, *to like or love*:

Vera houdt van Karel	*Vera loves Karel*
Karel houdt van tennis	*Karel likes tennis*
Vera houdt niet van sport	*Vera doesn't like sport*

Something you enjoy is **leuk**:

uitgaan is leuk	*going out is fun*
Nederlands leren is leuk	*learning Dutch is fun*

Leuk can also be used with **vinden** (= to think):

Peter vindt lezen leuk	*Peter likes to read*
hij vindt voetbal ook leuk	*he also likes soccer*

When you're talking about food you can also use **houden van**:

Marga houd van vis	*I like fish*
ik houdt niet van haring	*I don't like herring*

To describe your likes and dislikes you can also use the verb **lusten**, which is used exclusively with foods:

ik lust mosselen niet	*I don't like mussels*
ik lust mosselen wel	*I do like mussels*

Instead of **leuk** you have to use **lekker** to describe food. And if it's particularly nice you can use **heerlijk**:

de soep is lekker	*the soup is nice*
John vindt biefstuk lekker	*John likes steak*
ze vinden de patat heerlijk	*they love the chips*
ik vind de saus niet lekker	*I don't like the sauce*

The opposite of **lekker** is **vies**:

ik vind lever vies	*I hate liver*

Jan vindt bloedworst vies   *Jan hates black pudding*
wij vinden bloedworst niet vies   *we don't hate black pudding*

If you're hungry you can say **ik heb honger** and if you're only peckish you can say **ik heb trek**. If you feel like eating something in particular you can use **ik heb trek <u>in</u>**.

ik heb trek in een appel
I would like an apple
Marcel heeft trek in chocolade
Marcel feels like some chocolate

Order from a menu

As we saw in the dialogue, ordering from a menu in Dutch is pretty straightforward and is done in much the same way as in English, even though the menu may well turn out to be a little different!

De menukaart or **de kaart** lists all **gerechten** you can have in the restaurant. For **wijn** you have a look at **de wijnkaart**. When you've made your choice you call **de ober** who will take your **bestelling**.

As with ordering drinks and buying tickets the most straightforward way of ordering from a menu is simply saying what you want:

een fles witte huiswijn, graag
a bottle of house white, please
tomatensoep, alstublieft
tomato soup, please

Of course you can also use **ik wil . . .**:

ik wil de groentesoep en de biefstuk, alstublieft
I would like the vegetable soup and the steak, please

And **nemen**, literally *'to take'*, can be used to say what you will have:

ik neem tomatensoep   *I'll have tomato soup*
we nemen geen wijn   *we won't have wine*

If you're having dinner with others you can also use **voor mij . . .** to distinguish yourself from the others:

voor mij uiensoep, alstublieft
onion soup for me, please
voor mij hetzelfde, graag
for me the same, please

You might also want to indicate the course you're ordering:

ik neem de zalm als voorgerecht
I'm having the salmon as a starter

als hoofdgerecht neem ik de mosselen
I'm having mussels as my main course
als nagerecht wil ik ijs
I would like ice-cream for dessert

het voorgerecht	*the starter*
het hoofdgerecht	*the main course*
het nagerecht	*the dessert*

Instead of **voorgerecht** you can also use **vooraf**:

vooraf wil ik de kipsalade
I'm having the chicken salad to start with

And instead of **nagerecht** you can use **toe**:

ik neem ijs toe
I'm having ice-cream to finish

If you prefer something to something else you can use **liever**:

ik heb liever bloemkool
I would rather have cauliflower
Hans heeft liever tomatensoep
Hans would rather have tomato soup

STREETWISE

Restaurants in The Netherlands cater for a great many different tastes and a large number of foreign cuisines are available. The most popular of these are **Indonesisch** *Indonesian*, **Chinees** *Chinese*, **Italiaans** *Italian*, **Grieks** *Greek* and **Mexicaans** *Mexican*. Some ethnic restaurants are sometimes referred to by the name of the country's inhabitants: a Greek restaurant may be called **de Griek**, *the Greek*, for instance, and an Italian restaurant **de Italiaan**, *the Italian*. **Indonesisch** has been a long-standing favourite ever since the exotic spicy flavours of the Indonesian cuisine first reached the Dutch shores in colonial times. Many Dutch families now cook their own versions of traditional Indonesian dishes, especially **de rijsttafel**, rice with numerous side dishes.

A typical Dutch meal consists of **aardappelen** *potatoes*, **groente** *vegetables*, and **vlees** *meat*, sometimes mashed together into what is called **stamppot**. **Vis** *fish* is very popular, especially along the coast in the provinces of **Noord** and **Zuid Holland** and **Zeeland**. A particular favourite is **haring** *herring*, which is eaten raw. Another Dutch speciality is **de pannekoek**, *the pancake*, which may be topped with anything from ham and cheese to spinach and anchovy but which is typically eaten with nothing but **stroop** *syrup*.

Whether in a restaurant or at home, before starting a meal Dutch people always wish each other an enjoyable meal, **smakelijk eten**. During a meal they will ask **smaakt het?**, *are you enjoying the meal?*, and after the meal they will want to know **heeft het gesmaakt?**, *did you enjoy the meal?*

As in most other Western European countries **fooien**, *tipping*, is common practice in The Netherlands. **De fooi**, *the tip*, is usually expected to be about ten percent, although it's up to you to leave more (or less) if you thought the service was particularly good (or bad).

YOUR TURN

Exercise 1

Fill in the past participle of the verb given in brackets.

1. Heb je het journaal op tv . . .? (zien)
2. Het regent dus we zijn met de auto . . . (komen)
3. Hoe laat zijn jullie bij het hotel . . .? (aankomen)
4. Mijn vrouw heeft twee weken geleden . . . en een kamer . . . (opbellen/reserveren)
5. Een vriend heeft dit restaurant . . . (aanraden)
6. [**Ober** to customers:] Heeft u een keuze . . .? (maken)
7. Heb je het nieuwe boek van Atwood al . . .? (lezen)
8. Wanneer heb je het huis . . .? (kopen)

Exercise 2

Fill in the right forms of the separable verbs in brackets (present tense).

1. We . . . om vijf uur op Schiphol . . . (aankomen)
2. . . . je vanavond . . .? (uitgaan)
3. Welk restaurant . . . je . . .? (aanraden)
4. Ik . . . vanavond mijn ouders . . . (opbellen)

Exercise 3

Give your opinion about the following items in correct Dutch sentences. Some model answers are given in the key section, and more may be heard on the cassette.

bloemkool; voetbal; haring; sport; wijn; uitgaan; lezen; bier

Exercise 4

Finish the following sentences by putting the words given in brackets in the right order.

1. Als voorgerecht . . . (ik/zalm/wil)
2. Gisteren . . . (naar mijn werk/niet/ik/gegaan/ben)
3. Bij het eten . . . (ik/wijn/neem)
4. Na de film . . . (bed/ik/ga/naar)
5. Dit boek . . . (heb/gelezen/ik/niet)
6. Marina . . . (naar Hoorn/gaat/morgen)
7. Om half acht . . . (Henry en Eleonor/aan/komen/op Schiphol)
8. Vanavond . . . (ik/wil/naar de film)

WORD LIST

de aardappel	potato
bakken	to fry/bake
de biefstuk	steak
de brief	letter
de dame	lady
echt	really/truly
erg	very
de film	film
de fles	bottle
Frans	French
de friet	(French) fries
het gerecht	dish/course
gisteren	yesterday
de Griek	the Greek (man)
de groente	vegetable
heerlijk	delicious
hoewel	although
het hoofdgerecht	main course
de huiswijn	house wine
het ijs	ice/ice-cream
Italiaans	Italian
de kaart	menu
de keuze	choice
klinken	to sound
de koffie	coffee

lekker	nice (food)
lezen	to read
makkelijk	easy
Mexicaans	Mexican
moeilijk	difficult
de mossel	mussel
het nagerecht	dessert
de Noordzee	the North Sea
de ober	waiter
ongeveer	about / roughly
de patat	chips
reserveren	to make a reservation
de soep	soup
Turks	Turkish
vies	not nice (food)
de vis	fish
het visrestaurant	fish restaurant
het vlees	meat
het voorgerecht	starter

USEFUL EXPRESSIONS

aan tafel	at the table
eet (u) smakelijk	enjoy your meal
ik heb honger	I'm hungry
ik heb trek	I'm peckish
ik heb trek in ...	I feel like eating ...
in de buurt	nearby
om de hoek	around the corner
zeg het maar	you choose

KEY

Exercise 1

1. gezien; 2. gekomen; 3. aangekomen; 4. opgebeld/gereserveerd;
5. aangeraden; 6. gemaakt; 7. gelezen; 8. gekocht

Exercise 2

1. komen/aan; 2. ga/uit; 3. raad/aan; 4. bel/op

Exercise 3

These answers are only examples; there are many other possibilities.

1. Ik vind bloemkool lekker; 2. Ik houd niet van voetbal; 3. Haring is vies; 4. Ik vind sport leuk; 5. Ik vind wijn niet lekker; 6. Ik vind uitgaan leuk; 7. Ik houd van lezen; 8. Bier is heerlijk

Exercise 4

1. Als voorgerecht wil ik zalm; 2. Gisteren ben ik niet naar mijn werk gegaan; 3. Bij het eten neem ik wijn; 4. Na de film ga ik naar bed; 5. Dit boek heb ik niet gelezen; 6. Marina gaat naar Hoorn morgen/Marina gaat morgen naar Hoorn; 7. Om half acht komen Henry en Eleonor op Schiphol aan; 8. Vanavond wil ik naar de film

8 An Evening Out

Jessica is staying in Amsterdam for two weeks. She phones her Dutch friend Wim to arrange an evening out.

Wim:	Met Wim.
	Wim speaking.
Jessica:	Hoi Wim, met Jessica.
	Hi Wim, this is Jessica.
Wim:	Hoi Jessica. Wat leuk dat je belt! hoe gaat het met je?
	Hi Jessica. Nice to hear from you! How are you?
Jessica:	Prima en met jou?
	Very well, and yourself?
Wim:	Uitstekend, dank je.
	Excellent, thanks.
Jessica:	Luister, ik ben twee weken in Amsterdam. Heb je zin om van de week een avondje uit te gaan?

	Listen, I'm in Amsterdam for two weeks. Do you feel like going out one evening this week?
Wim:	Natuurlijk! Wanneer?
	Of course! When?
Jessica:	Morgen of donderdag?
	Tomorrow or Thursday?
Wim:	Hmm ... Mijn ouders hebben gevraagd of ik morgenavond bij ze kom eten en donderdagavond ga ik op visite bij Petra en Ben ... maar vrijdag kan ik wel.
	Well ... My parents have asked me for dinner tomorrow evening and Thursday evening I'm visiting Petra and Ben ... but I can do Friday.
Jessica:	Prima, ik kan vrijdagavond ook.
	Great, I can also do Friday night.
Wim:	Wat zullen we doen?
	What shall we do?
Jessica:	Wat je wilt. We kunnen gewoon gaan stappen, we kunnen uit eten, we kunnen naar een nachtclub of de bioscoop ...
	Whatever you like. We can just have a drink, we can have a meal, we can go to a nightclub or the cinema ...
Wim:	Ja, zullen we naar de bioscoop gaan?
	Yes, shall we go to the cinema?
Jessica:	Ja leuk, ik ben al lang niet naar de bioscoop geweest. Welke film wil je gaan zien?
	Yes that would be nice. I haven't been to the cinema for a long time. What film would you like to see?
Wim:	Wil je de nieuwste James Bond zien?
	Do you want to see the latest James Bond film?
Jessica:	Ja, ik heb gehoord dat het een spannende film is.
	Yes, I've heard that it's really exciting.
Wim:	Misschien is het een goed idee om plaatsen te reserveren omdat het op vrijdagavond altijd erg druk is.
	Perhaps it would be a good idea to reserve tickets because it's always very busy on Friday nights.
Jessica:	Ja, ik zal morgen even langs de bioscoop rijden om kaartjes te kopen.
	Yes, I'll go past the cinema tomorrow to buy the tickets.

Wim:	Waar spreken we af?
	Where shall we meet?
Jessica:	Het maakt me niet uit.
	It's all the same to me.
Wim:	Bij wie slaap je deze twee weken?
	Who are you staying with these two weeks?
Jessica:	Bij Miriam in de Celebesstraat. Ik pas op haar huis terwijl zij op vakantie is.
	At Miriam's, in the Celebesstraat. I'm house-sitting for her while she's on holiday.
Wim:	Nou, dan haal ik je bij haar op en dan gaan we daar vandaan eerst naar café Vermeer om iets te drinken.
	Well, then I'll pick you up from her place and from there we'll go to Vermeer bar first to have a drink.
Jessica:	Prima. Hoe laat zullen we afspreken?
	Great. What time shall we say?
Wim:	Hoe laat begint de film denk je?
	What time do you think the film starts?
Jessica:	Meestal om een uur of negen.
	Usually around nine.
Wim:	Zullen we dan om half acht afspreken?
	Shall we make it half past seven then?
Jessica:	Okee.
	OK.
Wim:	Nou, tot vrijdagavond.
	Well, see you Friday night.
Jessica:	Tot dan!
	See you then!

HOW IT WORKS

WELKE DAG IS HET?

Here are the days of the week:

maandag	*Monday*	**vrijdag**	*Friday*
dinsdag	*Tuesday*	**zaterdag**	*Saturday*
woensdag	*Wednesday*	**zondag**	*Sunday*
donderdag	*Thursday*		

Note that the days of the week are not written with capitals in Dutch.

The following may also come in useful:

gisteren	*yesterday*
morgen	*tomorrow*
eergisteren	*the day before yesterday*
overmorgen	*the day after tomorrow*
volgende week	*next week*
verleden week	*last week*

Een dag is divided into four parts:

de ochtend/morgen	*the morning*
de middag	*the afternoon*
de avond	*the evening*
de nacht	*the night*

In chapter 5 we learnt that *in the morning, in the afternoon*, etc. is: **'s ochtends/morgens, 's middags, 's avonds, 's nachts**. When talking about **vandaag** you should use:

vanmorgen/vanochtend	*this morning*
vanmiddag	*this afternoon*
vanavond	*this evening*
vannacht	*tonight*

If you want to refer to a particular day and time, *Thursday afternoon* for instance, you can join the two different words and make a new word: **donderdagmiddag**. Likewise you can make: **vrijdagochtend, maandagnacht, morgenavond, woensdagmorgen**, etc. **Gisteren** is irregular in this respect because it loses its **-en** ending in these cases: **gistermorgen, gistermiddag** etc.

POSSESSION

Here's how we say that something belongs to us or someone else:

<u>**mijn**</u> **ouders**	<u>*my*</u> *parents*
<u>**haar**</u> **huis**	<u>*her*</u> *house*

Dutch uses these words in exactly the same way as English, except that there are different stressed and unstressed forms:

singular:	stressed	unstressed	
	mijn	**(m'n)**	*my*
	jouw	**je**	*your* (informal)
	uw	–	*your* (formal)
	zijn	**(z'n)**	*his/its*
	haar	**(d'r)**	*her*
plural:	**ons/onze**	–	*our*
	jullie	**je**	*your* (informal)
	uw	–	*your* (formal)
	hun	–	*their*

Ons is used for **het** words and **onze** is used for **de** words:

het huis	**ons huis**
de auto	**onze auto.**

The unstressed forms in brackets are considered rather colloquial and are therefore not normally used in written Dutch; they merely give an indication of the pronunciation of these forms.

Another way of indicating possession in English is by using *'s*: *Peter's house*. This can also be done in Dutch, except that you don't use an apostrophe, only an **s**: **Peters huis.** However, it is much more common in these cases to use . . . **van** . . . Here are some examples:

het huis van Bernhard	*Bernard's house*
de hond van Maaike	*Maaike's dog*
de auto van Piet en Marie	*Piet and Marie's parents*

IK – MIJ – ME, JIJ – JOU – JE

We know that it is possible in sentences like **Joost belt Jeroen** and **Sharon belt Jannie** to replace **Joost** and **Sharon** with **hij** and **zij**:

hij belt Jeroen	*he calls Jeroen*
zij belt Jannie	*she calls Jannie*

Just as we could replace **Joost** and **Sharon**, we can also replace **Jeroen** and **Jannie**:

hij belt hem	*he calls him*
zij belt haar	*she calls her*

As you can see, we have to use different words in this case, as in English; instead of **hij** and **zij** we use **hem** and **haar**. The difference is that **Joost** and **Sharon** are the subjects of the sentences above and **Jeroen** and **Jannie** are not.

To distinguish between a subject and a non-subject you could say that a subject actively does something and that the non-subject is on the receiving end of whatever is being done. (Joost and Sharon are making the calls, while Jeroen and Jannie are receiving the calls.)

Both in English and in Dutch subjects and non-subjects are referred to by using different words. A subject can be **hij** *he* or **zij** *she* but a non-subject would be **hem** *him* or **haar** *her*. In the following examples from the dialogue the non-subjects are underlined:

hoe gaat het met je?
het maakt me niet uit
dan haal ik je bij haar op
... of ik bij ze kom eten

Here are all the different forms for non-subjects (for subjects see chapter 3):

	stressed	unstressed	
singular	**mij**	**me**	*me*
	jou	**je**	*you* (informal)
	u	–	*you* (formal)
	hem	**('m)**	*him*
	haar	**(d'r)**	*her*
	het	**('t)**	*it*
plural:	**ons**	–	*us*
	jullie	–	*you* (informal)
	u	–	*you* (formal)
	hun/hen	**ze**	*them* (people)
	ze	–	*them* (things)

Note that the forms in brackets are spoken forms, which aren't used in writing. The difference between **hen** and **hun** is rather complicated, even to Dutch people, and nowadays most people simply use **ze** in all cases, particularly in speech.

The following situation illustrates the difference between the stressed and unstressed forms:

Caroline meets Cora, a friend, and asks how she is doing: **hoe gaat het met je?** (unstressed). When Cora answers she says **goed, en met jou?** Cora uses **jou**, the stressed form, in order to distinguish between herself and Caroline (in English the stress would be the same: *How are you?* and *Very well, and how are you?*).

It may sound strange to English speaking ears but Dutch people refer to things and animals not only as **het** but also as **hij/hem**.

de auto staat in de garage	*the car is in the garage*
hij staat in de garage	*it is in the garage*
ik repareer de fiets	*I'm repairing the bicycle*
ik repareer hem	*I'm repairing it*
het huis is groot	*the house is big*
het is groot	*it is big*

As you can see, **hij/hem** is used to refer to **de** words and **het** is used to refer to **het** words. Sometimes **ze/zij** and **haar** are used to refer to animals that are known to be female (often by pet-owners when they're talking about their pet):

de poes slaapt	*the cat is sleeping*
ze slaapt	*it is sleeping*

TALKING ABOUT THE FUTURE

There are different ways of talking about the future. The easiest way is to use the same form of the verb as you do when talking about the present. Often you will use words like **morgen** or **volgende week** to indicate you're referring to the future. This is done in English as well (see the first example below), but in Dutch it is much more common:

ik ben morgen thuis
I am at home tomorrow / I will be at home tomorrow
ik doe het volgende week
I'll do it next week

Another way of talking about the future is by using **gaan**, as in English. You must remember to use the correct form of **gaan**, depending on the subject of the sentence (see chapter 5), and to place the infinitive at the very end of the sentence, for instance:

ik ga morgen 'Just enough Dutch' kopen
I am going to buy 'Just Enough Dutch' tomorrow
we gaan eerst iets drinken
we're going to have a drink first

A third, more emphatic, way of talking about the future is by using **zullen**, *shall* and *will* in English. We have already been using this verb:

zullen we iets drinken?
shall we have a drink?

Here are the other forms of **zullen**.

singular:
ik zal
jij zult/zal
u zult/zal
hij/zij/het zal

plural:
wij zullen
jullie zullen
u zult
zij zullen

Zult and **zal** mean the same thing and can be interchanged freely. As with **gaan**, the second verb used with **zullen** is an infinitive, placed at the very end of the sentence. Here are some more examples with **zullen**:

ik zal mijn kamer morgen opruimen
I'll clean up my room tomorrow
Janet zal je aanstaande maandag bellen
Janet will call you next Monday

OM ... TE ...

Several times in the dialogue you will have come across the structure **om ... te ...**

heb je zin <u>om</u> een avondje uit <u>te</u> gaan?
do you feel like going for an evening out?

we gaan naar café Vermeer <u>om</u> iets <u>te</u> drinken
we're going to have a drink at Vermeer bar

As you can see from these examples, the **om ... te ...** structure expresses a purpose or intention to do something: **om uit te gaan**, *to go out*, or **om iets te drinken**, *to go and have a drink*.

The examples also show that **te** is always followed by an infinitive, so the whole structure looks like this:

om ... te + infinitive

Te + inf is always placed at the end of the sentence. Here are some more examples:

het is een goed idee om plaatsen te reserveren
it's a good idea to reserve seats

ik ben uitgenodigd om te komen eten
I've been invited to come for dinner (lit.: 'to come eat')

The last example shows that **te** can also be followed by more than one verb (all of them infinitives).

THE DUTCH CONNECTION (II)

In the previous chapter we saw that two sentences can be linked together by words such as **en**, **of**, **maar**, **want** and **dus**:

het eten is lekker maar de wijn is vies
the food is nice but the wine isn't

Maar is placed between the two sentences **het eten is lekker** and **de wijn is vies**, and one longer sentence is made.

Now have a look at the following sentence from the dialogue:

ik pas op haar huis terwijl zij op vakantie is
I'm house-sitting for her while she's on holiday

In this case the two sentences **ik pas op haar huis** and **zij is op vakantie** are linked together by **terwijl**. The difference here is that the word order of the second sentence changes: the verb **is** is moved to the end of the sentence.

There is a whole group of link words which have this effect. They move the verb or verbs in the second sentence to the end of the sentence. Here are some more examples from the dialogue (the linking words are underlined and the verb that is moved is in italics):

ik heb gehoord <u>dat</u> het een spannende film *is*
I've heard that it's an exciting film

misschien is het een goed idee om te reserveren <u>omdat</u> het op vrijdagavond altijd erg druk *is*
perhaps it's a good idea to make a reservation because it's always very busy on Friday nights

mijn ouders hebben gevraagd <u>of</u> ik morgenavond bij ze <u>kom</u> eten
my parents have asked whether I'll come for dinner tomorrow evening

Note that in the first sentence **dat** cannot be left out unlike *that* in English. In the last sentence, **of** means *whether*. If **of** means *or*, as in the previous chapter, word order does not change.

Omdat means the same as **want** but only **omdat** can be used to answer as question starting with **waarom** . . .? *why. . .?*

A: **Waarom blijf je thuis vandaag?**
   Why are you staying home today?
B: **Omdat ik ziek ben.**
   Because I'm ill.

Other linking words that affect word order are:

als	*when*	. . . **als ik rijk ben**
wanneer	*when*	. . . **wanneer ik rijk ben**
hoewel	*although*	. . . **hoewel ze rijk is**

HOW TO ...

Ask how someone is

informal:

hoe gaat het met je?	*how are you?*
hoe maak je het?	*how are you?*

formal:

hoe gaat het met u?	*how are you?*
hoe maakt u het?	*how are you?*

informal and formal:

hoe gaat het?	*how are you?*
hoe is het?	*how are you?*

Answer the phone

The major difference between answering the phone in English and in Dutch is that in Dutch you answer by **met** + your name.

The most informal way of answering the phone is by saying your first name only: **met Koos**. The more formal way is to say both your first and last names: **met Koos Kaart**. Even more formal is answering with your last name only, **met Kaart**, or adding **meneer/mevrouw**: **met meneer Kaart**.

Next, the person who is calling also says his or her name in the same way: **met** ... From here the conversation can go many ways, depending on why the call is being made. Here are some useful phrases:

is ... er?
is ... there?

is ... thuis?
is ... at home?

kan ik ... spreken?
can I talk to ...?

mag ik toestel ...?
extension ... please

moment(je), graag
one moment, please

ogenblik, graag
one moment, please

het spijt me, ... is er niet
I'm sorry, ... isn't here

het spijt me, ... is niet thuis
sorry, ... isn't at home

kan ik een boodschap achterlaten?
can I leave a message?

STREETWISE

There are, of course, countless ways of spending an evening out, but the most truly Dutch way is going to **het bruin café**. **Een bruin café**, literally *'a brown café'*, is a traditional Dutch pub, usually with wooden floors, walls, ceilings, tables and chairs, where the main aim is **gezelligheid**; creating a good atmosphere. The traditional drink to have here, besides **bier**, *beer*, is **jenever**, the Dutch ancestor of English gin. Going out for an evening to one or more pubs is called **gaan stappen**, *to go out for drinks*. Such an evening does not usually start before nine o'clock and can last well into the small hours.

Recently another type of **café** has become more popular, **het grand café**. **Een grand café** is much larger and lighter in décor than **een bruin café**, with comfortable furniture and stylish designs. In a **grand café** you can usually also eat meals and they are particularly popular for tea and coffee.

As snacks to go with a drink the Dutch serve the usual **pinda's** *peanuts*, and **chips** *crisps*, but they also serve **kaas** *cheese* and **bitterballen**, small deep-fried balls filled with a kind of ragoût.

Another popular way of spending an evening out is going to **de bioscoop**, *the cinema*. Foreign **films** in The Netherlands are never dubbed but are given **ondertitels**, *subtitles*. You can therefore go and see any English or American film without fear, although you should be prepared for **de pauze**, *interval*, in the middle of the film. **De pauze** doesn't necessarily occur at an appropriate moment in the film, but at least it gives you another opportunity to relieve yourself and get a drink and some more popcorn . . .

Listings of all kinds of cultural events can be found in the national newspapers (for the larger cities) or in local publications, such as **de Uitkrant** in Amsterdam.

YOUR TURN

Exercise 1

Answer the questions by looking at **de agenda van Caroline**
(answer in full sentences):

maandag	dinsdag	woensdag	donderdag
			9⁰⁰ zwemmen
	15⁰⁰ koffie met		
	Mark		
20⁴⁵ bioscoop			

vrijdag	zaterdag	zondag	
	11⁰⁰ boodschappen		
		16⁰⁰ Jogger met	
		Marie	
20⁰⁰ eten			
bij Jannie			

1. Wanneer gaat Caroline boodschappen doen?
2. Wanneer gaat Caroline naar de bioscoop?
3. Met wie gaat Caroline dinsdag koffie drinken?
4. Hoe laat gaat Caroline donderdag zwemmen?
5. Bij wie gaat Caroline vrijdag eten. Hoe laat?
6. Op welke dag gaat Caroline joggen. Hoe laat?

Exercise 2

Fill in the gaps.

1. Ik kan ... (*my*) sleutels niet vinden.
2. Marie heeft ... (*her*) tas verloren.
3. Heb je ... (*our*) nieuwe auto al gezien?
4. Martijn heeft ... (*his*) sleutels vergeten.
5. ... (*our*) huis heeft drie slaapkamers.
6. Mag ik ... (*your*, informal) vakantiefoto's zien?

Exercise 3

Replace the underlined names:

1. Heb je Willem al gebeld?
2. Ik heb gisteren bij Hans en Margriet gegeten.
3. Morgen ga ik met Petra naar de bioscoop.
4. Mijn vader gaat met de hond naar de dierenarts.
5. Margo weet het nieuws nog niet.

Exercise 4

Make into one sentence:

1. Caroline belt Joachim/Ze is thuis/Als
2. Joan en Hendrik willen naar huis/Ze zijn moe/Omdat
3. Theo zei/Annemarie is op vakantie/Dat
4. Ik zal haar bellen/Ze is terug van vakantie/Wanneer
5. Bea heeft gevraagd/Ik wil met haar uit eten/Of

WORD LIST

afspreken	(to arrange) to meet
de agenda	diary
de bioscoop	cinema
de dierenarts	veterinarian
druk	busy
de fiets	bicycle
gaan stappen	to go out (for a drink)
gewoon	ordinary/just
de hond	dog
het huis	house
het idee	idea
joggen	to jog
het kaartje	ticket
leuk	nice/fun
maar	but
meestal	usually
de nachtclub	nightclub
natuurlijk	naturally/of course
het nieuws	(piece of) news
nog niet	not yet
de ouder	parent
de plaats	seat/place
de poes	cat
rijden	to drive/ride
rijk	rich
slapen	to sleep

spannend	exciting
de tas	bag
terug	back
terwijl	while
thuis	at home
uitstekend	excellent
welk(e)	which
ziek	ill
zwemmen	to swim

USEFUL EXPRESSIONS

het maakt me niet uit	it's all the same to me
tot dan!	see you then!

KEY

Exercise 1

1. Caroline gaat zaterdagmorgen om elf uur boodschappen doen;
2. Caroline gaat maandagavond om kwart voor negen naar de bioscoop; 3. Caroline gaat dinsdag met Mark koffie drinken;
4. Caroline gaat donderdagochtend om negen uur zwemmen;
5. Caroline gaat vrijdag bij Jannie eten, om acht uur 's avonds;
6. Caroline gaat zaterdag joggen, om vier uur 's middags.

Exercise 2

1. mijn; 2. haar; 3. onze; 4. zijn; 5. ons; 6. je/jouw

Exercise 3

1. hem; 2. ze; 3. haar; 4. hem; 5. het

Exercise 4

1. Caroline belt Joachim als ze thuis is; 2. Joan en Hendrik willen naar huis omdat ze moe zijn; 3. Theo zei dat Annemarie op vakantie is; 4. Ik zal haar bellen wanneer ze terug van vakantie is;
5. Bea heeft gevraagd of ik met haar uit eten wil

9 A Day Out

Charles and Janet want to spend a day out of town and are looking for the tourist information office, **de VVV**, to get some more information about where they could go. They can't find the office so they ask a passer-by.

Charles: Pardon mevrouw, weet u waar het VVV-kantoor is?
Excuse me, do you know where the VVV office is?

Passer-by: Ja hoor. Ziet u dat gebouw aan de overkant, naast die bloemenzaak? Dat is het VVV-kantoor.
Certainly. Can you see that building across the road, next to that florist's? That's the VVV office.

Charles: Dank u wel.
Thank you.

Inside the **VVV-kantoor** Janet asks one of the assistants, **de medewerker**, for information.

Janet: We willen een dagje de stad uit. Heeft u suggesties?
We'd like to get out of the city for the day. Do you have any suggestions?

Medewerker: Nou, u kunt naar de kust, in het westen. Daar kunt u een strandwandeling maken. Of u kunt verder weg, een dagje naar het zuiden, naar Limburg, bijvoorbeeld. Er zijn tal van mogelijkheden.
Well, you can go to the West Coast. You can take a walk along the beach there. Or you could go further away, a day in the south, in Limburg, for instance. There are numerous possibilities.

Janet: We zijn al naar het strand geweest en ook naar Limburg. Het is misschien leuker om deze keer iets anders te doen.
We've been to the beach already and also to Limburg. Perhaps it'd be nicer to do something else this time.

Medewerker: U kunt ook een dagje naar de Veluwe, een natuurgebied meer naar het oosten, rond Arnhem.
You could also go to the Veluwe for a day, a nature reserve more to the east, around Arnhem.

Janet: Is dat dichtbij?
Is that close by?

Medewerker: Het is ongeveer een uur met de trein. Het is een van de mooiste natuurgebieden van Nederland en je kunt er goed fietsen.
It's about an hour by train. It's one of the most beautiful areas in The Netherlands and it's very nice to cycle around.

Janet: We hebben helaas geen fietsen.
We don't have bicycles, unfortunately.

Medewerker: O, maar u kunt fietsen huren.
Oh, but you can hire bicycles.

Janet: Waar kan dat?
Where?

Medewerker: Dat kan bij de meeste grote NS-stations.
At most large railway stations.

Charles: Is het wel een goed idee met kinderen? Misschie
is het te vermoeiend voor onze jongste zoon.
*Would it be a good idea with children? Perhaps it wou
be too tiring for our youngest son.*

Medewerker: Voor kinderen zijn er natuurlijk speciale
kinderfietsen en de fietspaden op de Veluwe zij
erg goed. Hoe oud is uw jongste?
*Naturally there are special bicycles for children and the
cycle paths in the Veluwe are very well maintained.
How old is your youngest?*

Janet: Hij is vijf en een half.
He's five and a half.

Medewerker: Misschien is het dan handiger om voor hem een
kinderzitje te nemen.
*Perhaps it's more practical in that case to put him in a
child's seat.*

Charles: Denkt u dat het weer wel goed genoeg is om te
fietsen?
Do you think the weather is good enough to go cycling

Medewerker: De weersverwachting voor vandaag is redelijk:
bewolkt maar niet veel wind, niet koud en slecht
een kleine kans op regen. Prima fietsweer!
*The weather forecast is reasonable for today: cloudy but
not too windy, not cold and only a small chance of rain
Excellent cycling weather!*

Charles: Nou, als het maar droog blijft. Toen we verleden
week op het strand waren, zijn we kletsnat
geworden.
*Well, as long as it stays dry. When we went walking
last week we got soaked.*

Janet: Moeten we de fietsen van tevoren reserveren?
*Should we make reservations for the bicycles
beforehand?*

Medewerker: In het hoogseizoen wel maar nu, in het voorjaar,
is dat niet nodig. Je moet jezelf wel dubbel
legitimeren en een borg achterlaten, dus u moet
uw paspoort en rijbewijs meenemen en wat extra
geld.

You should in the high season but now, in the spring, it
won't be necessary. You do have to take two forms of
identification and leave a deposit, so you should take
your passport and driving licence and some extra
money.

Charles: Heeft u een kaart van de Veluwe?

Do you have a map of the Veluwe?

Medewerker: Nee, in dit kantoor niet. In het VVV-kantoor in
Arnhem kunt u meer informatie over de Veluwe
krijgen.

*No, not in this office. At the VVV office in Arnhem
you'll be able to get more information about the Veluwe.*

Janet: Vriendelijk bedankt.

Thank you very much.

Medewerker: Geen dank. Een prettige dag!

You're welcome. Have a nice day!

HOW IT WORKS

DE MAANDEN VAN HET JAAR

In the previous chapter we learnt the days of the week; now
we'll have a look at the months of the year:

januari	*January*	**juli**	*July*
februari	*February*	**augustus**	*August*
maart	*March*	**september**	*September*
april	*April*	**oktober**	*October*
mei	*May*	**november**	*November*
juni	*June*	**december**	*December*

Note that **de maanden** are written without capitals in Dutch.

There are **vier seizoenen** *four seasons* in The Netherlands:

de lente	*Spring*
de zomer	*Summer*
de herfst	*Autumn*
de winter	*Winter*

De lente can also be called **het voorjaar** and **de herfst** is sometimes called **het najaar**.

There are two different seasons for holiday makers:

het hoogseizoen	*high season*
het laagseizoen	*low season*

DAT GEBOUW – DIE BLOEMENZAAK

Have a look at this sentence from the dialogue:

ziet u <u>dat</u> gebouw aan de overkant, naast <u>die</u> bloemenzaak?
can you see that building across the road, next to that florist's?
As you can see, **dat** and **die** both mean *that*. **Dat** is used for **het** words and **die** is used for **de** words. There are also two words for *this*: **dit** and **deze**. **Dit** is used for **het** words and **deze** for **de** words.

	this	*that*
het words:	**dit**	**dat**
de words:	**deze**	**die**

Some examples:

het kantoor	*the office*	**de fiets**	*the bicycle*
dit kantoor	*this office*	**deze fiets**	*this bicycle*
dat kantoor	*that office*	**die fiets**	*that bicycle*

Remember that all plural words are **de** words, so:

deze kantoren	*these offices*
deze fietsen	*these bicycles*
die kantoren	*those offices*
die fietsen	*those bicycles*

Dit, **dat**, **deze** and **die** can also be used on their own when it is clear what you're talking about.

A: **Welke CD neem je?**	B: **Ik neem die.**
A: *Which CD are you taking?*	B: *I'm having that one.*

As you can see, you usually add *one* in English in these situations.

When you want to describe or identify something or someone you can also use **dit** and **dat**:

dit is mijn vader *this is my father*
dat is mijn moeder *that is my mother*

In these cases **deze** and **die** are never used. **Dit** and **dat** are also used in the plural:

dit zijn mijn zusters *these are my sisters*
dat zijn mijn broers *those are my brothers*

COMPARISONS

When comparing two things which aren't equal, the following happens:

het strand is leuk **de Veluwe is leuker**
the beach is good fun *de Veluwe is more fun*

een fiets is handig **een kinderzitje is handiger**
a bicycle is practical *a child's seat is more practical*

You simply add **-er** to **leuk** and **handig** to say something is more fun and more practical. This goes for all descriptive words:

mooi	*beautiful*	**mooier**	*more beautiful*
koud	*cold*	**kouder**	*colder*
groot	*big*	**groter**	*bigger*
duur	*expensive*	**duurder**	*more expensive*
lekker	*nice*	**lekkerder**	*nicer*
ver	*far*	**verder**	*further*

Note that an extra **d** is added to words ending in **-r**: **ver/verder, duur/duurder, lekker/lekkerder**. And don't forget to apply the spelling rules discussed in chapter 1: **groot/groter**.

Remember that the rules for adding an **-e** to descriptive words (see chapter 4) still apply:

het huis **een mooi huis** **een mooier huis**
the house *a beautiful house* *a more beautiful house*

de auto **een mooie auto** **een mooiere auto**
the car *a beautiful car* *a more beautiful car*

When comparing things you will also encounter extremes:

het jongste kind   *the youngest child*
het mooiste gebied   *the most beautiful area*

In such cases you add **-st** to the descriptive word:

koud	*cold*	**koudst**	*coldest*
groot	*big*	**grootst**	*biggest*
duur	*expensive*	**duurst**	*most expensive*
lekker	*nice*	**lekkerst**	*nicest*
ver	*far*	**verst**	*furthest*

Words ending in **-s** only add a **-t**:

fris	*fresh*	**frist**	*most fresh*

The rules for adding an **-e** also apply here, but since you will not use this kind of description with **een** (you're always talking about a specific object, which is by definition always **de** or **het**), you needn't worry and you can always add an **-e**:

het mooiste huis   *the most beautiful house*
de leukste vakantie   *the best (most fun) holiday*

As usual, there are also a few important irregular forms. These you will simply have to learn by heart:

goed	*good*	**beter**	*better*	**best**	*best*
weinig	*little*	**minder**	*less*	**minst**	*least*
veel	*many*	**meer**	*more*	**meest**	*most*

TOEN

In the previous chapter we saw that **als** and **wanneer** both mean *when*. In this chapter we see the following:

toen we verleden week op het strand waren . . .
when we were on the beach last week . . .

Toen also means *when*. The difference with **als** and **wanneer** is that **toen** is only used to talk about the past.

Toen is used with a form of the verb **gaan** which you haven't encountered before: **gingen** *went*. This form is called the simple past. In English it is used quite often but in Dutch it is used mainly after **toen**.

Because the simple past is not used so frequently when speaking Dutch, we won't waste any time on the rules for making this tense. We'll only have a look at the simple past forms of the verbs you are most likely to come across. For each verb there is a form for the singular (**ik/jij/u/hij/zij/het**) and the plural (**wij/jullie/zij**).

verb (infinitive)	singular	plural	
zijn	**was**	**waren**	*was/were*
hebben	**had**	**hadden**	*had*
gaan	**ging**	**gingen**	*went*
doen	**deed**	**deden**	*did*
worden	**werd**	**werden**	*became*
krijgen	**kreeg**	**kregen**	*got*
zien	**zag**	**zagen**	*saw*
moeten	**moest**	**moesten**	*must*

Some examples:

toen ik verleden jaar in Maastricht was . . .
when I was in Maastricht last year . . .
toen we naar de Efteling gingen was het mooi weer
it was beautiful weather when we went to the Efteling
toen ik vijf werd kreeg ik een fiets
when I turned five I got a bike

HOW TO ...

Talk about the weather, **het weer**

There is often a strong **wind** in The Netherlands, which can blow from four directions, **de windrichtingen: het noorden, het oosten, het zuiden, het westen.**

het is mooi weer	*it's nice weather*
het is droog	*it's dry*
het is warm	*it's warm*
de zon schijnt	*the sun is shining/it's sunny*
het is 23 graden	*it's 23 degrees* (always Celsius)
het is slecht weer	*the weather's bad*
het regent	*it's raining*
het is koud	*it's cold*
het is bewolkt	*it's cloudy*
het waait	*it's windy*
het sneeuwt	*it's snowing*
het hagelt	*it's hailing*
er is mist	*it's foggy*
het vriest	*it's freezing*

STREETWISE

There is a wealth of beautiful places to visit and interesting things to do outside the major cities in The Netherlands. There is the coast in the west, the islands in the north, the lakes in the province of **Friesland**, caves in the south, etc., etc. An added advantage is that all of this is never more than a few hours' travel away and generally extremely easy to reach by public transport.

For all kinds of tourist information you can contact **het VVV**, the national tourist information bureau. **Het VVV** has branches in most towns and provides information about accommodation, transport, opening hours, prices and anything else you might want to find out, and also sells maps and information booklets of the local area.

De NS, the Dutch railway company, offers special day-trip arrangements, which include a return train ticket and the entrance fee to wherever you are going, which may be anything from a museum to a theme park. A special booklet listing all these daytrips can be picked up from any railway station.

If travelling by car you can get information from **de ANWB**, the Dutch automobile association. **De ANWB** has branches in most larger cities and sells maps, brochures and information booklets (both for domestic and foreign destinations) and offers advice and help regarding your car.

Road maps can also be bought from most **tankstations**, *petrol stations*. **Tankstations** can be found along major roads at regular intervals and often also sell food and drink. Petrol is called **benzine** in Dutch and comes in **normaal**, *normal*, **super** and **loodvrij**, *unleaded*. Diesel and LPG are simply called **diesel** and **LPG**.

YOUR TURN

Exercise 1

Fill in **dit**, **deze**, **die** or **dat**, as appropriate.

1. Van wie is . . . jas hier?
2. Zie je . . . grote kantoor daar?
3. . . . koffie is lekkerder dan de koffie van Karin.
4. Ik vind . . . pak mooier dan . . . pak.
5. Wil je hier eten of wil je terug naar . . . andere restaurant?
6. Zag je . . . jongen aan de overkant van de straat?
7. Ik had . . . film nog nooit gezien.
8. . . . tentoonstelling is interessanter dan . . . andere.

Exercise 2

Fill in the right form of the words in brackets.

1. Dit boek is . . . dan dat boek. (beautiful)
2. Ik vind dit schilderij het . . . (beautiful)
3. Johanna vindt vis . . . dan vlees. (nice)
4. Mijn auto is . . . dan jouw auto. (big)

5. Het is in Zweden . . . dan in Nederland maar het is op de Noordpool het . . . (cold)
6. Ik drink . . water dan whisky. (rather)
7. In Amsterdam wonen . . . mensen maar in New York wonen . . . mensen. (many)
8. Dit concert is . . . dan het concert verleden jaar. (good)

Exercise 3

Give the simple past form of the verb.

1. Toen we verleden jaar naar Parijs (gaan), (zijn) het mooi weer.
2. Ik (doen) de deur dicht en toen (zien) ik dat het slecht weer (zijn).
3. Ik (zijn) tot 8 uur op mijn werk want ik (moeten) nog veel doen.
4. Toen ik klein (zijn), (hebben) we twee honden thuis.
5. Met de kerst (krijgen) we allemaal cadeaus van mijn ouders.
6. Op het vliegveld (moeten) we onze koffers openmaken.

WORD LIST

de bloemenzaak	florist's
de broer	brother
de deur	door
droog	dry
het fietspad	cycle path
het gebied	area
het geld	money
genoeg	enough
handig	handy/practical
helaas	unfortunately
huren	to rent
de informatie	information
de jas	coat
de kaart	map
het cadeau	present
de kans	chance
het kantoor	office
de kerst	Christmas
het kind	child
de kinderen	children
de kinderfiets	children's bicycle
de koffer	suitcase
koud	cold

de kust	coast
de medewerker	assistant/staff member
de moeder	mother
de mogelijkheid	possibility
nat	wet
het natuurgebied	nature reserve
het NS-station	railway station
openmaken	to open
de overkant	the other side
het pak	suit
het paspoort	passport
redelijk	reasonable
de regen	rain
het rijbewijs	driving licence
rond	round/around
het schilderij	painting
het strand	beach
de strandwandeling	walk along the beach
de suggestie	suggestion
tal van	numerous
de tentoonstelling	exhibition
de vader	father
van tevoren	beforehand
het vliegveld	airport
het weer	weather
de weersverwachting	weather forecast
het werk	work
de zoon	son
de zus(ter)	sister

USEFUL EXPRESSIONS

geen dank	you're welcome
vriendelijk bedankt	thank you very much

KEY

Exercise 1

1. deze; 2. dat; 3. deze (die); 4. dit, dat; 5. dat; 6. die; 7. die (deze); 8. deze, die

Exercise 2

1. mooier; 2. mooist; 3. lekkerder; 4. groter; 5. kouder, koudst; 6. liever; 7. veel, meer; 8. beter

Exercise 3

1. gingen, was; 2. deed, zag, was; 3. was, moest; 4. was, hadden; 5. kregen; 6. moesten

10 Shopping

Karen is on holiday, **op vakantie**, in The Netherlands and she wants to do some shopping. She meets up with her Dutch friend Ronald in town, **in de stad**.

Karen: Hoi Ronald.
Hi Ronald.

Ronald: Hoi Karen. Hoe gaat het met je?
Hi Karen. How are you?

Karen: Prima, en met jou?
Very well, and you?

Ronald: Ook prima.
I'm well, too.

Karen: Dank je wel dat je me wilt helpen met het winkelen.
Alleen winkelen vind ik nooit leuk.
Thanks for wanting to help me with my shopping. I never like shopping on my own.

Ronald: Niets te danken. Winkelen vind ik altijd leuk. Wat wil je kopen?

You're very welcome. I always like shopping. What do you want to buy?

Karen: Ik wil cadeaus voor mijn familie kopen en misschien ook iets voor mezelf.

I want to buy presents for my family and perhaps something for myself.

Ronald: Laten we eerst ergens een kopje koffie nemen, dan kunnen we tijdens de koffie bespreken waar we naartoe moeten.

Let's go and have a coffee somewhere first, then we can discuss where to go over coffee.

Karen: Een goed idee.

That's a good idea.

During coffee, **tijdens de koffie**.

Ronald: Voor wie wil je cadeaus kopen?

Who do you want to buy presents for?

Karen: Voor m'n vader en moeder, m'n broer, m'n zusje en voor m'n oma.

For my father and mother, my brother, my sister and my grandmother.

Ronald: Dat is niet niks! Heb je al enig idee wat je wilt kopen?

That's quite a lot! Have you any idea what you want to get them [what you want to buy]?

Karen: Ik dacht voor m'n vader en moeder een Delfts blauw bord.

I thought about a Delft blue plate for my father and mother.

Ronald: Daarvoor moeten we naar een speciaalzaak waar ze porselein en aardewerk verkopen.

For that we'll have to go to a special shop china and pottery shop.

Karen: En m'n oma is gek op Hollandse kaas, dus ik wil een groot stuk kaas voor haar kopen met een kaasschaaf.

And my gran loves Dutch cheese, so I'd like to buy a large piece of cheese with a cheese slicer for her.

111

Ronald: Dan kunnen we het beste naar een kaaswinkel gaan, daar hebben ze keuze genoeg.
Then we'd best go to a cheese shop, plenty of choice there.

Karen: M'n broer en zusje zijn een beetje een probleem want ik weet niet wat ik voor ze moet kopen.
My brother and little sister are a bit of a problem because I don't know what to get them.

Ronald: Houdt je broer van voetbal?
Does your brother like soccer?

Karen: O ja, hij is een grote fan.
Oh yes, he's a great fan.

Ronald: Dan kun je misschien een voetbal-shirt van een Nederlandse club voor hem kopen. Van Ajax of Feijenoord, bijvoorbeeld?
Perhaps you can buy him a soccer shirt from a Dutch club then. Ajax or Feijenoord, for instance?

Karen: Waar kunnen we zo'n shirt krijgen?
Where can we get a shirt like that?

Ronald: Bij een sportzaak.
In a sports shop.

Karen: Dan alleen nog iets voor mijn zuster.
And then only something for my sister.

Ronald: Hoe oud is ze?
How old is she?

Karen: Ze is twaalf.
She's twelve.

Ronald: Misschien kunnen we in een van de grote warenhuizen gaan kijken. Dan komen we vast wel op een idee.
Perhaps we can have a look in one of the large department stores. That is sure to give us some ideas.

Karen: Ja goed, dan kan ik ook voor mezelf rondkijken.
Very good, then I'll be able to have a look for myself as well.

Ronald: Moet je anders nog iets?
Is there anything else you need?

Karen: Alleen nog een paar ansichtkaarten.
Only a few postcards.

In a cheese shop, **in een kaaswinkel**.

Verkoper: Wie is er aan de beurt?
Who's next?

Karen: Ik.
I am.

Verkoper: Zegt u het maar.
What'll it be?

Karen: Ik wil een stuk oude kaas, alstublieft.
I'd like a piece of mature cheese, please.

Verkoper: We hebben verschillende soorten, wilt u proeven?
We have different kinds, would you like to taste them?

Karen: Ja graag . . . Hmm. Deze is het lekkerst. Wat is dit voor kaas?
Yes please . . . Hmm. This one is the nicest. What kind of cheese is this?

Verkoper: Dit is Goudse kaas.
This is Gouda.

Karen: Doet u dan maar anderhalf pond Goudse kaas.
Make that a pound and a half of Gouda, please.

Verkoper: Het is iets meer.
It's a little over.

Karen: Dat is prima.
That's fine.

Verkoper: Anders nog iets?
Anything else?

Karen: Ja, ik zoek ook een kaasschaaf, verkoopt u die?
Yes, I'm also looking for a cheese slicer, do you sell those?

Verkoper: Jazeker. Anders nog iets?
Certainly. Anything else?

Karen: Nee dank u, dat was het.
No thanks, that's it.

Verkoper: Dat is negentien gulden vijfenzeventig bij elkaar.
That's nineteen guilders and seventy-five cents altogether please.

HOW IT WORKS

MIJN ZUSJE

It is common in Dutch to add the ending **-je** to words. You've probably noticed **een dagje uit**. In this lesson, we meet **zusje** and **kopje**. The basic meaning added by **-je** is *little* but it is often used to make a word sound nicer. Sometimes the **-je** ending becomes a permanent feature, e.g. **een broodje** *a sandwich roll*.

Because the **-je** ending can be hard to pronounce after certain words variations on **-je** also occur. Here are some examples:

de boom	het boompje	*tree*
de broer	het broertje	*brother*
de man	het mannetje	*man*
de woning	het woninkje	*flat*

These examples show that all words with the **-je** ending or a variation are **het** words.

Dutch people are extremely fond of the **-je** ending and like to use it often, so don't be surprised to find it even after a word like **de berg** *the mountain*: **het bergje**!

WEIGHTS AND MEASURES

anderhalf pond Goudse kaas

All weights in Dutch are in grams and kilos. Weights are always singular: **10 kilo** and **100 gram** without the plural **-s**. Note that the Dutch **pond** is different from the British *pound*:

100 gram	=	het ons
500 gram	=	het pond
1000 gram	=	de kilo

Have a look at the following weights and measures:

een halve kilo appels	*half a kilo of apples*
twee liter melk	*two litres of milk*
twee kopjes thee	*two cups of tea*
een doos bonbons	*a box of chocolates*
een glas wijn	*a glass of wine*

Note that in Dutch you don't use an equivalent of the English *of*. Unlike weights, other measures can become plural:

de doos   **3 dozen bonbons**
het glas   **4 glazen wijn**

However, **liter** is always singular.

FAMILY AND FRIENDS

Here are the main family relations in Dutch:

de vader
father

de moeder
mother

de zoon
son

de dochter
daughter

de broer
brother

de zus(ter)
sister

de oom
uncle

de tante
aunt

de neef
nephew/cousin

de nicht
niece/cousin

de grootvader/opa
grandfather

de grootmoeder/oma
grandmother

Oma and **opa** are the equivalents of *grandma* and *grandpa*. **Vader** and **moeder** together are **de ouders**. There are also several endearing terms for **vader** and **moeder**. **Vader** is usually called **papa/pappa** by children, or **pap** or **pa** especially when the children are a little older. Likewise **moeder** is called **mama/mamma**, or **mam** or **ma**.

Unmarried people have **een vriend of vriendin** or, if their relationship is more established, **een partner**.

In-laws are **de schoonouders** or **de schoonfamilie**:

de schoonvader
father-in-law

de schoonmoeder
mother-in-law

de schoonzoon
son-in-law

de schoondochter
daughter-in-law

de zwager	**de schoonzus(ter)**
brother-in-law	*sister-in-law*

And relatives from another marriage are:

de stiefvader	**de stiefmoeder**
stepfather	*stepmother*
de stiefzoon	**de stiefdochter**
stepson	*stepdaughter*
de stiefbroer	**de stiefzus(ter)**
stepbrother	*stepsister*

You will find that Dutch children often call their parents by their first names and address them as **je** but that **opa** and **oma** are often still **u**, although this is changing gradually. Most other members of the family, like **oom** and **tante**, are also often called by their first names by the **jongere generaties**.

A REMINDER

In chapter 3 we saw that the **-t** ending of verbs after **je** or **jij** is lost whenever the verb is moved in front of **je** or **jij**:

je bent ziek	**ben je ziek?**
you're ill	*are you ill?*

In this chapter we come across the following sentence:

houdt je broer van voetbal?   *does your brother like soccer?*

At first it may seem strange that the **-t** ending of the verb remains, but if we take a closer look at the sentence it does make sense. In the earlier sentences **je** meant *you* (the weak form of **jij**) but in this last sentence **je** means *your* (the weak form of **jouw**). The **-t** ending of a verb is lost only if the verb is followed by **je** when this **je** is the weak form of **jij**.

VERDIEPINGEN

It won't always be easy to find your way around big stores, particularly **het warenhuis** *the department store*. To help you find your way, have a look at the following vocabulary:

de verdieping	*floor*
de begane grond	*ground floor*
de eerste verdieping	*first floor*
de tweede/derde, etc. verdieping	*2nd/3rd floor*
de kelder	*basement/cellar*

Different departments or **afdelingen** are **op de begane grond/eerste verdieping**, etc., but **in de kelder**. To move between floors you can use the stairs, the escalator or the lift:

met de trap	*by stairs*
met de roltrap	*by escalator*
met de lift	*by lift*

Here are some departments which it might be useful to know:

de damesmode	*ladies' fashion*
de herenmode	*men's fashion*
huishoudelijke artikelen	*household goods*
elektrische apparaten	*electrical appliances*

And if it all becomes too much you can always head for **het restaurant** or **de koffieshop**.

HOW TO ...

Make your wishes known

When you're shopping you will often be able to simply take things from the shelves, but sometimes you will have to ask for things. Some of the vocabulary needed for this has been seen in previous chapters, but there are also several new structures.

You may be asked who's next or what you want:

wie is er aan de beurt?	*who's next?*
kan ik u helpen?	*can I help you?*
zegt u het maar	*can I help you?/what'll it be?*

Some ways to indicate what you're after:

ik zoek . . .	*I'm looking for . . .*
heeft u . . .?	*do you have . . .?*
verkoopt u . . .?	*do you sell . . .?*
waar kan ik . . . vinden?	*where can I find . . .?*

To say what you're having:

ik wil . . .	*I'd like . . .*
mag ik . . .	*may I have . . .?*
[produkt] graag/alstublieft	*[product] please*
doet u maar . . .	*make that . . . please*
zou ik . . . mogen?	*could I have . . .?*

You may then be asked the following:

anders nog iets?	*anything else?*
dat was het?	*that was it?*

And the possible answers are obvious enough:

ja, . . .	*yes, . . .*
nee dank u	*no thanks*
nee, dat was het	*no, that was it*

Don't forget to say **alstublieft** when handing over the money and to say **bedankt** or **dank u wel** when receiving your change back.

STREETWISE

The Dutch like to do their shopping on a small scale in specialist **winkels**, *shops*. They prefer to buy their **boodschappen**, *groceries*, for instance, in small **buurtwinkels** *neighbourhood shops*, if possible. You will therefore find countless small greengrocer's, butcher's and corner stores in most town centres. Supermarkets can mostly be found outside the centre of town in the suburbs, and usually have separate fresh vegetable, meat and bread sections. The best known chain of supermarkets is **Albert Heijn**.

Warenhuizen, *department stores*, do exist but there are only a few large ones. As in most western European high streets a large number of the same chains of shops appear in every town. The best-known chains with a wide selection of household goods, and in the case of the first two also a choice of other goods, are **de Hema**, **Vroom en Dreesman** and **Blokker**. Some shops will be familiar to UK citizens. C&A has outlets in most towns and Marks & Spencer have opened shops in several large cities.

De openingstijden, *opening hours*, are roughly the same for most stores: they usually open between 9 and 9.30 a.m. and close between 6 and 7 p.m. Recently, opening hours have become less restrictive. Most towns have a designated **koopavond**, one evening a week on which shops are allowed to stay open until 9 p.m., which is usually Thursday. In most large towns you will also find *night shops*, **de nachtwinkel**, so there is no need to panic if you get a late-night craving for chocolate, crisps or **bitterballen**.

YOUR TURN

Exercise 1

Provide appropriate responses in the following dialogue: You're food-shopping in a Dutch town and you try a small food store, **een kruidenierswinkel**.

kruidenier: Goedemorgen, kan ik u helpen?

you:	1. [you greet back and say you want 2 litres of milk]
kruidenier:	Volle of halfvolle melk?
you:	2. [you want half fat milk]
kruidenier:	Anders nog iets?
you:	3. [ask for 10 eggs]
kruidenier:	Anders nog iets?
you:	4. [you'd also like 500 grams of 'young' cheese]
kruidenier:	Goudse kaas of Edammer?
you:	5. [you prefer the Edam cheese]
kruidenier:	Dat was het?
you:	6. [yes that's all]
kruidenier:	Dat is zestien gulden vijftig.
you:	7. [you hand the shopkeeper a 25 guilder note]
kruidenier:	Dank u wel. Met acht vijftig wisselgeld.
you:	8. [thank **de kruidenier** and ask him if he knows where to find a **groenteboer** *greengrocer's*]
kruidenier:	Ja hoor. U moet hier rechts en dan neemt u de eerste straat links. Er is een groenteboer aan uw rechterhand.
you:	9. [thank him for his information and greet him before leaving]

Exercise 2

The following sentences all contain word(s) which have been given a special ending to convey the fact that they are meant to be small and/or likeable. Remove the endings to find the original words (if you have a Dutch dictionary to hand, also check whether it's a **het** or a **de** word).

1. We hebben een hondje gekocht.
2. Annie wil een feestje geven op haar verjaardag.
3. Wil je een of twee schepjes suiker?
4. Er zijn erg veel leuke winkeltjes hier in de buurt.
5. Heb je dat mannetje nooit eerder gezien?
6. Wil je een kopje thee? Nee, ik heb liever een drankje.
7. Carola en Dik spelen vadertje en moedertje.
8. Heb je het nieuwe vriendinnetje van Bas al gezien?

Exercise 3

In een kledingzaak

Put the following sentences in the right order to make up a dialogue between **een klant** and **een verkoper/verkoopster**.

Weet u wat voor soort broek u wilt?
Ja, prima. Ze zitten alletwee goed.
Ja, goedemorgen. Ik zoek een broek.
Ik heb hier een bruine en een zwarte. Wilt u ze passen?
Goedemorgen, kan ik u helpen?
Ja graag.
Zitten ze goed?
Ik neem ze alletwee.
Ik wil een bruine of een zwarte spijkerbroek.
Welke neemt u?

WORD LIST

alleen	alone/only
alletwee	both
anderhalf	one and a half
de ansichtkaart	postcard
de berg	mountain
bespreken	to discuss
de boom	tree
het bord	plate
de broek	trousers
bruin	brown
het drankje	alcoholic drink
de Edammer kaas	Edam cheese
de familie	family
het feest	party
de generatie	generation
de Goudse kaas	Gouda cheese
de groenteboer	greengrocer's
de halfvolle melk	half-fat milk
jazeker	certainly/yes
de kaas	cheese
de kaasschaaf	cheese slicer
de klant	customer
de melk	milk
nooit	never
de oma	grandma
de oom	uncle
de opa	grandpa
op een idee komen	to get an idea
passen	to try on/to fit (clothes)
proeven	to taste
de roltrap	escalator
rondkijken	to look around
de schep	spoonful
de speciaalzaak	speciality shop

de spijkerbroek	jeans
de sportzaak	sports shop
de tante	aunt
tijdens	during
de verdieping	floor (story)
de verkoopster	saleswoman
de verkoper	salesman
verschillend	different
voetbal	soccer
de volle melk	full-fat milk
het warenhuis	department store
het wisselgeld	change (money)
de woning	flat/house
zitten	to sit/fit (clothes)

USEFUL EXPRESSIONS

dat is niet niks	that's quite something
hoe gaat het met je?	how are you doing?
niets te danken	you're (very) welcome

KEY

Exercise 1

Remember these answers are only examples. 1. Goedemorgen, twee liter melk alstublieft; 2. Halfvolle melk graag; 3. Tien eieren alstublieft; 4. Ik wil ook een pond jonge kaas graag; 5. (Ik heb liever) Edammer alstublieft; 6. Ja, dat was het; 7. Alstublieft; 8. Dank u wel. Weet u waar ik een groenteboer kan vinden?; 9. Vriendelijk bedankt. Tot ziens.

Exercise 2

1. de hond; 2. het feest; 3. de schep; 4. de winkel; 5. de man; 6. de kop, de drank; 7. de vader, de moeder; 8. de vriendin.

Exercise 3

verkoper: Goedemorgen, kan ik u helpen?
klant: Ja, goedemorgen. Ik zoek een broek.
verkoper: Weet u wat voor soort broek u wilt?
klant: Ik wil een bruine of een zwarte spijkerbroek
verkoper: Ik heb hier een bruine en een zwarte. Wilt u ze passen?
klant: Ja graag.
verkoper: Zitten ze goed?
klant: Ja, prima. Ze zitten alletwee goed.
verkoper: Welke neemt u?
klant: Ik neem ze alletwee.

Mini-Dictionary

A
de aardappel potato
de accommodatie accommodation
achterin at the back
de achternaam last name
de afslag turning
afspreken (to arrange) to meet
afstempelen to stamp
de agenda diary
het alfabet alphabet
alleen alone/only
alletwee both
anderhalf one and a half
de ansichtkaart postcard
het appelsap apple juice
de auto car

B
het bad bath
de badkamer bathroom
bakken to fry/bake
het balkon balcony
de bank bank
de benzine petrol
de berg mountain
bespreken to discuss
betalen to pay
de biefstuk steak
het bier beer
het biertje one beer
bijna nearly/almost
de bioscoop cinema
de bloemenzaak florist's
het boek book
de boom tree
het bord sign/plate
de borg deposit
de brief letter
het briefje note
de brievenbus post box
de broek trousers

de brug bridge
bruin brown
de bus bus
de busdienst bus service
het busstation bus station
de buurtwinkel neighbourhood shop

C
het cadeau present
het café café/bar/pub
de camping camp site
de chauffeur driver
de chips crisps
de creditcard credit card

D
de dame lady
Den Haag The Hague
de deur door
dichtbij nearby
de dierenarts vet(erinary)
de douane customs
de douche shower
het drankje alcoholic drink
droog dry
druk busy

E
echt really/truly
de Edammer kaas Edam cheese
de eenpersoonskamer single room
Engeland England
Engels English
de enkele reis single ticket/journey
het enkeltje single ticket
erg very
exclusief excluding

F
de familie family
het feest party

de fiets bicycle
het fietspad cycle path/lane
de film film
de fles bottle
de fooi tip
fooien to tip
Frans French
de friet (French) fries

G
gaan stappen to go out (for a drink)
de gang corridor
het gebied area
het gebouw building
het geld money
de geldautomaat cash-dispensing
  machine
de generatie generation
genoeg enough
het gerecht dish/course
gewoon ordinary/just
de Giromaat cash-dispensing
  machine
gisteren yesterday
de Goudse kaas Gouda cheese
de gracht canal
de grens border
de Griek the Greek (man)
  Grieks Greek
de groente vegetable
de groenteboer greengrocer's
de gulden guilder

H
de halfvolle melk half-fat milk
de halte the stop (public transport)
handig handy/practical
de haring herring
heerlijk delicious
helaas unfortunately
hoewel although
de hond dog
het hoofdgerecht main course
het huis house
de huiswijn house wine
huren to rent

I
het idee idea
het ijs ice/ice-cream
inclusief including
Indonesisch Indonesian
de informatie information
de intercity fast train
Italiaans Italian

J
ja yes
de jas coat
jazeker certainly/yes
de jeugdherberg youth hostel
joggen to jog
jong young

K
de kaart menu/map
het kaartje ticket
de kaas cheese
de kaasschaaf cheese slicer
de kamer room
de kans chance
de kantoor office
de kerk church
de kerst Christmas
de keuze choice
het kind child
de kinderen children
de kinderfiets children's bicycle
de klant customer
klein small
klinken to sound
de klok clock
de koffer suitcase
de koffie coffee
  koffiedrinken to drink coffee
  het kopje koffie cup of coffee
  de koffie verkeerd milky coffee
kopen to buy
koud cold
de kust coast
het kwartje 25 cent coin

L
lang long/tall
lekker nice (food)

124

leuk nice/fun
lezen to read
het loket counter
de lokettist(e) man/woman behind
  counter
Londen London
loodvrij unleaded

M
maar but
makkelijk easy
meestal usually
de melk milk
meneer sir
de metro the underground
mevrouw madam
Mexicaans Mexican
het mineraalwater mineral water
moe tired
moeilijk difficult
de mogelijkheid possibility
mooi beautiful
morgen tomorrow
de mossel mussel
de munt coin

N
de naam name
naar to
de nacht night
  de nachtbus night bus
  de nachtclub nightclub
  de nachttrein night train
  de nachtwinkel (all-)night shop
het nagerecht dessert
nat wet
het natuurgebied nature reserve
natuurlijk naturally/of course
Nederland The Netherlands
  Nederlands Dutch
nieuw new
het nieuws news
nog niet not yet
nooit never
de Noordzee the North Sea
normaal normal
de NS Dutch railway company
het NS-station railway station

O
de ober waiter
de oma grandma
de ondertitel subtitle
ongeveer about/roughly
het ontbijt breakfast
ook also
de oom uncle
de opa grandpa
op een idee komen to get an idea
de openingstijden opening hours
openmaken to open
oud old
de ouder parent
de overkant the other side

P
het pak suit
de pannekoek pancake
het paspoort passport
passen to try on/to fit (clothes)
de patat chips
de pauze break
het perron platform
de persoon person
de pinda peanut
de plaats seat/place
de plattegrond map
de poes cat
het pond pound
het postkantoor post office
de postzegel stamp
precies exactly
prima very well/fine
de prijs price
het probleem problem
proeven to taste

R
redelijk reasonable
de regen rain
reserveren to make a reservation
de reservering reservation
het restaurant restaurant
het rijbewijs driving licence
rijden to drive/ride
rijk rich
de roltrap escalator

rond round/around
rondkijken to look around
de rotonde roundabout

S
de schep spoonful
het schilderij painting
slapen to sleep
de sleutel key
de sneltrein fast train
de soep soup
spannend exciting
de speciaalzaak speciality shop
de spijkerbroek jeans
de sportzaak sports shop
het station station
de stempelautomaat ticket-stamping machine (public transport)
het stoplicht traffic lights
de stoptrein slow train
de straat street
het strand beach
de strandwandeling walk along the beach
de strippenkaart ticket for public transport
de stroop syrup
de suggestie suggestion
de suiker sugar
de supermarkt supermarket

T
tal van numerous
het tankstation petrol station
de tante aunt
de tas bag
de televisie television
de tentoonstelling exhibition
terug back
terwijl while
te veel too much
het theater theatre
thuis at home
de tijd time
tijdens during
het toilet toilet
de tram tram
de trap stairs

de trein train
  de treindienst train service
Turks Turkish
tv kijken to watch TV
de tweepersoonskamer double room

U
uit eten gaan to go out for dinner
uitstappen to get off
uitstekend excellent

V
de vakantie holiday
vandaag today
van tevoren beforehand
veel many
ver far
de verdieping floor (story)
de verkoopster saleswoman
verkopen to sell
de verkoper salesman
verschillend different
de vertrektijd time of departure
vies not nice (food)
de vis fish
het visrestaurant fish restaurant
vlakbij close (by)
het vlees meat
het vliegveld airport
voetbal soccer
de volle melk full-fat milk
het voorgerecht starter
de vriend (boy)friend
de vriendin (girl)friend

W
wachten to wait
wachten op to wait for
het warenhuis department store
de wasmachine washing machine
de wedstrijd match/game
het weer weather
de weersverwachting weather forecast
welk(e) which
het werk work
de wijn wine

de **windrichting** point of the
  compass
de **winkel** shop
winkelen to shop
wisselen to change (items, money,
  etc.)
het **wisselgeld** change (money)
de **woning** flat/house

Z
het **zebrapad** zebra crossing
ziek ill
de **zijstraat** sidestreet
de **zone** zone
de **zoon** son
zwart black
zwemmen to swim

USEFUL EXPRESSIONS

aan de overkant across/on the other
  side
aan tafel at the table
bent u/ben je hier bekend? do you
  know the area?
dank u wel thank you
dat is niet niks that's quite
  something
een prettige vakantie! have a nice
  holiday!
eet (u) smakelijk enjoy your meal
er is ... there is ...
er zijn... there are ...
geen dank you're welcome
goedemiddag good afternoon
goedemorgen good morning
goedenavond good evening
heeft het gesmaakt? did you enjoy
  the meal?
het maakt me niet uit it's all the
  same to me
het spijt me I am sorry
hoe gaat het met je? how are you
  doing?
hoeveel kost de kamer? how much
  does the room cost?
hoe laat ...? what time ...?
ik ben verdwaald I'm lost
ik heb honger I'm hungry
ik heb trek I'm peckish
ik heb trek in ... I feel like eating
  ... (food)
ik wil graag ... I would like ...

in de buurt nearby
in huis in the house
ja graag yes please
kan ik u helpen? can I help you?
kun je dat spellen? can you spell
  that?
kunt u/kun je me helpen? can you
  help me?
mag ik u/je iets vragen? may I ask
  you something?
met bad/douche/toilet with
  bath/shower/toilet
mijn geld is op I've run out of
  money
mijn naam is ... my name is ...
niets te danken you're welcome
om de hoek around the corner
op het station at the station
per nacht per night
per persoon per person
prettig kennis te maken pleased to
  meet you
smaakt het? are you enjoying the
  meal?
tot dan! see you!
de **trein is vertrokken** the train has
  left
u heeft de trein gemist you have
  missed the train
vriendelijk bedankt thank you very
  much
zeg het maar you choose
zonder bad/douche/toilet without
  bath/shower/toilet

Index